Camp Sights

Sam Cook

Illustrations by Bob Cary

University of Minnesota Press
Minneapolis • London

Grateful acknowledgment is made to the *Duluth News-Tribune* for permission to reprint these stories and columns, which originally appeared in that newspaper.

Originally published in hardcover by Pfeifer-Hamilton, 1992

First University of Minnesota Press edition, 2002

Published by the University of Minnesota Press
111 Third Avenue South, Suite 290
Minneapolis, MN 55401-2520
http://www.upress.umn.edu

A Cataloging-in-Publication record for this book is available from the Library of Congress.

ISBN 0-8166-4184-6

Printed in the United States of America on acid-free paper.

12 11 10 09 08 07 06 05 04 03 02   10 9 8 7 6 5 4 3 2

For Grant

Acknowledgments

Many people deserve credit and thanks for helping make this book happen. I deeply appreciate my partner and wife, Phyllis, for her continued support of my work. She inspires some of it. She offers candid commentary. She holds the home front together when I'm on the trail. She's a wonderful companion, both in the woods and in town.

Many of these stories and essays first appeared in the Duluth News-Tribune, *with whose permission they are gathered here. I thank the* News-Tribune *for allowing the work to be reprinted and for its commitment to outdoor coverage. My editors have given me a lot of freedom, both in traveling and in expressing my opinions, and I appreciate that.*

Bob Cary brings authenticity and the spirit of the North Country to this book with his illustrations. But beyond that,

I find him an inspirational character. His wit, his energy, and his perspective on life have helped shape my own.

Inspiration and encouragement have come from many camps, including traveling companions and good friends. I appreciate the insights and support of David Spencer, Steve Harrington, Bob Ashenmacher, Ken Gilbertson, and many others.

I thank Jim Brandenburg for introducing me to arctic wolves on Ellesmere Island. I thank Dave Olesen for some fine traveling behind good dogs on the fringes of Great Slave Lake. I appreciate all of the people with whom I've shared campsites and fishing boats and portage trails. I am thankful for living in good country, full of good people.

S. C.
Duluth, Minnesota

Contents

Spring

Summer

Fall

Winter

CampSights

Camp.

You know the place. You know the feeling that fills you when you're there. You're free and in touch with the rhythm of the land.

In camp everything is right. The way the evening light plays on the far ridge. The way the firelight dances on faces of good friends. The way the morning sun warms your arms as you paddle away.

Maybe it's a canoe camp on a shoulder of granite, waiting for your tent and campfire. Or a duck camp in October's gold. Or a deer camp in a spruce hollow.

You slow down when you get to camp. You begin to notice the little things again—a shift in the wind, fresh tracks, the angle of the sun.

And when it's time to leave, you come away with a new perspective. Humility is part of it. An appreciation for the simple life. And simply feeling right with the world again.

Spring

The Bobber

This story began when my wife came home with the bobber.

She'd been out walking, and she came in and set the bobber on the table. It was a little yellow and red job—the standard item.

"Here's a bobber," she said. "I found it."

Already having an ample supply of bobbers myself, I told our five-year-old that she could have it. She was excited about that. But then it occurred to me she had no place to put it.

"We ought to get you a tackle box," I said.

"Yeah, I want my own tackle box," she said. "Can we get it today?"

I was tickled that she liked the idea. Already I was

embracing this—getting her first tackle box—as something of a rite of passage.

She'd already caught her share of sunfish, a couple of bass and a northern pike. Well, the northern got off right at the boat, but it was the biggest fish she'd almost ever caught, and she hasn't forgotten it. Neither have I.

And now, her own tackle box.

At the bait shop, she knew just what she was looking for. When the man pulled out a shoe-box size Flambeau tackle box with a handle on the top and a clasp on the front, she was ready to have me write the check. "That's the kind I want," she said. "Sarah has one like that."

It was made of beige plastic, and on the inside it had a slotted tray that lifted up on little plastic arms.

Thinking of all the portage trails I'd be lugging this tackle box over during the next few years, I tried to steer her toward a smaller box. But, no. She wanted the Flambeau with the handle and the tray.

Seven dollars later it was ours.

When we got it home, she was off and about, taking it to her room and hauling it over to Sarah's. I didn't know just what she was putting in it, but I did notice that the bobber was still on the dining room table.

I saw the tackle box in the corner of the living room one night, about a week after the box became part of the family. My daughter was asleep. I thought I'd have a look.

The first thing I noticed was that she had drawn flowers and sky and trees and a smiling face on top of the tackle box. That was good. I would have no trouble telling it from mine.

I opened it.

Once the lid was up the contents expanded, like a goosedown sleeping bag being freed from its stuff sack.

The tray held only one item—a tube of a child's pretend lipstick. I lifted the tray and sorted through the rest of the goodies. In no particular order, here's what I found that my girl had stashed in her first tackle box:

A pink doll outfit. A pair of her own shorts. Two Bic pens. A roll of Scotch tape. A foot-long piece of red licorice. A pad of paper imprinted with the words *Things To Do Today*. An L.A. Gear fanny pack.

There's more.

A container of Johnson's Baby Powder. A tube of strawberry lipstick. An L.A. Gear key chain. A flowered, metal saucer. Five rocks from Arizona. Another pad of paper.

Carefully, I stowed all of the contents back into the tackle box, trying to replace them in the correct order so the shorts and the doll outfit would be near the top.

I smiled.

This was seven bucks well-spent. She loves that tackle box.

Someday, she might even put the bobber in it.

Steelhead Alarm

Getting up early is a vice habitual in horned owls,
stars, geese and freight trains. Some hunters acquire
it from geese, and some coffee pots from hunters.
Aldo Leopold, *A Sand County Almanac*

The shattering noise came from somewhere in another world. It pounded my head until it finally intruded into my consciousness. In desperate retaliation I flailed an arm over the side of the bed and beat the alarm clock into silence.

I looked at the cruel red numbers on the clock: 3:15.

On another day, I might have tried to rationalize five more minutes of sleep. But not today. Not with an obligation to pick up a fishing buddy at 4:00 A.M.

We were going to head for a nearby river to fish for

steelhead, the migratory rainbow trout that ascend Lake Superior's tributaries each spring.

I staggered to an upright position and tugged on layers of insulation. I slugged down some Wheat Chex, but wondered why. Does a person need breakfast in the middle of the night? And if he eats one, when does he eat lunch? At 7:30? And if he does that, when does he eat supper? And is he then out of sync for the rest of his life, or what?

I didn't have time to wait for the answers.

The car knew the way to my buddy's house, where I found him not only awake but out on the curb in his hip boots, trying to read the morning paper by street light.

I must make two things clear here. First, we could not legally fish until 5:10 A.M. Second, we were not headed for Canada or any other far-flung destination. We were bound for a river about four Top 40 songs on the car radio from my buddy's house.

But my pal takes no chances. We had gotten up in the middle of the night to insure that we would get the spot we wanted when we arrived at the river.

"I got up at 2:30 to go fishing one time," he said.

Nothing like sleeping in until 3:15, I say.

I remember how we had decided to leave at 4:00 A.M. We knew the sun would rise at 6:10 A.M. We knew we could legally fish an hour before that—at 5:10. So I suggested I pick him up at about 4:15.

"That's what I was thinking," he had said. "And if it's 4:15, it might as well be 4:00, huh?"

We left at 4:00.

My buddy has been steelhead fishing long enough to know what it means to arise in the middle of the night, make a thermos of coffee, drive to a river and find someone in your favorite hole. That's why he almost always subtracts 15 minutes—or more—from the logical rising time.

Might as well make sure, he figures.

This same man has been known to set the timer on his watch when he arrives at the river, to see by how much he beats his closest competition. One morning, farther up the shore, he had beaten a couple of fellow anglers to a hole by about half an hour.

The next morning, expecting to see them on the river again, he set his alarm 15 minutes earlier. He beat them by five minutes.

Walleye and bass anglers rarely must scheme so precisely. They fish on lakes. There's plenty of room on lakes.

But fish concentrate in rivers, and anglers concentrate on fish. And most river anglers have a sweet spot they prefer over all others.

We arrived at an empty parking lot—a good sign. I had to slip into my chest waders. It must have seemed like an eternity to my buddy. He had worn his waders from home.

Once I was ready, we made tracks for the river. It was still pitch black. A full moon was riding the western sky toward moonset. All around was the sound of the river.

I have followed men possessed before. I know all the signs. The long strides. The branches in the face. The tangles of a fly rod in balsam boughs. The wrong trail taken in haste. The brush-crashing shortcut to the right path. My buddy had them all.

Finally, we arrived at the spot. We were alone. We had made it.

We were half an hour too early to fish, but we were

in position. Not only were we alone at our hallowed hole, but we were alone on the river—at least so far as we could see in the moonlight.

But we weren't finished worrying. We staked out our spots about 30 feet apart. Then my partner joined me at my spot. We poured cups of coffee and hot chocolate.

We tried to enjoy them, sitting there on the rocks, listening to the river. But I noticed that my buddy kept looking over his shoulders, first one way, then the other. He was looking for other anglers. He couldn't relax.

"I've had people sneak in behind me," he said.

We tossed down the last of our hot drinks and became fully territorial. We went to the river. We took up our rods. We waited for legal fishing time.

At 5:10, we began fishing. We were still alone—alone with the river and the moonlight and the rhythm of our downstream drifts.

Before the morning was gone, my buddy hooked three fish. Two got off quickly. The third must have been five or six pounds. My friend played the fish to the slack water at the side of the river, but the steelhead flipped off the hook before he could claim it.

Near as I could tell, the next angler arrived about an hour after we had begun fishing. He didn't want our hole. He fished across the river.

But the lighter the morning grew and the better I could see the other fisherman, the more I was sure of it.

He had a certain look about him. A look of peace. A look of calm. The look of a man who had gotten a decent night's rest.

Harriet's Rock

If you were following her down London Road on her
way out of Duluth, you'd figure she was heading up the
Shore, a little woman, up in years, out in her rustless
1984 Oldsmobile for a lakeshore tour.

All you can see of her from your vantage point is a
few gray curls sprouting above the headrest. Yep. A
senior citizen, out for coffee at the Lakeview Castle or
maybe meeting friends at the Harbor House in Two
Harbors.

Nope.

Not Harriet Schwenk.

The Oldsmobile was just across the Lester River on
this morning in May when it peeled off London Road
and took up occupancy in the first parking lot on the
right. It has made this stop a few hundred times before.

Harriet Schwenk, 72, was going fishing.

"I'm heading for my favorite rock," she said.

She was toting an 8 1/2-foot shorecasting rod in one hand and a landing net bulging with fishing gear and extra clothes in the other. She had drawn a bead on a lump of basalt that protrudes from a pebble beach just east of the Lester River.

"It's my rock," she announced. "If anybody else is on it, that's not good."

You might have seen Schwenk heaving her Little Cleos and Woblures and Krocodiles into Lake Superior. "I try to come down every day," she said. "I say I'm going to come down for an hour, but it's always an hour and a half or two hours. One last cast, you know."

If you were to see her, you would likely not forget her. She is a mite of a woman.

"I used to be 4-foot-9 1/2, but now I'm 4-8 1/2," she said.

Her weight, she said, is "under a hundred pounds."

But watch her fling the orange and gold hammered spoon into that big blue lake and you can tell that the woman knows her business.

She grabbed that 8 1/2-foot Kunan rod with both hands, issued a warning to stand clear of her backcast and whipped the rod in the general direction of Cornucopia.

The lure hissed into the wind, finally yielding to gravity 30 or 40 yards out. She began cranking her old Mitchell 300A reel, and hoping.

"Boy, I'd like to get a nice big one," she said. "But that isn't easy."

It has happened, however. Last fall, from the same rock, she landed a 10-pound Kamloops rainbow trout. She also caught four salmon the same month—October.

Not that all outings are successful.

"You should have been here the other day," she said. "I had a six- or seven-pounder up here"—she pointed at the rocks near her feet—"right in this hollow. But I fell down trying to get it. Got completely soaked."

The salmon got away.

Often, she said, men fishing nearby will help her net a fish, and one time a tourist from Tennessee who had been watching from his car came down to assist her.

"But every time I get a big one, I'm down here alone," she said.

Schwenk and her husband, George, used to fish from a boat on Lake Superior. When George's health failed, he would sit in the car and watch his wife shorecast at the Lester.

"If I had trouble with my line, he'd bring my other pole down," she said.

George died several years ago. Harriet has kept fishing. When she isn't at the Lester, she's tending her garden or taking a neighbor's dog for a walk or putting out a fresh orange for the Baltimore orioles.

She's in bed by 9:00 most nights, up at 5:30 each morning, and out doing her two-mile walk at 6:30. She knows how to laugh. She doesn't take herself or the world too seriously.

She carries her extra tackle—two or three lures, some scissors, two snap-swivels—in one of those red and black boxes that the bank sends new checks in. In an hour and a half of fishing on this day, she won't go to her "tackle box" once.

"I never change my lure," she said. "I don't change unless I lose one."

Midway through her morning session of casting, her

friend Al Dahlquist stopped by. He, too, is a shore-caster, although he had done his fishing earlier in the morning.

Schwenk will fish at or before dawn, too, but only if she knows Dahlquist is fishing. It's a security issue.

"He says, 'If my truck is gone from my driveway, you go,' " Schwenk said.

She remembered one day she was going to do that. She had set her alarm clock for 5:00 A.M. It was a new clock, because her old one had failed her the previous morning. This happened in October, when the world is dark at 5:00 A.M. Well, her new alarm went off, and Schwenk got up to go fishing.

"It was bitter cold. I wore my snowsuit," she said. "I drove by (Dahlquist's) and his truck was sitting there. I thought, well, I'll go home and give him half an hour."

Which she did.

"I had my breakfast and washed some cukes (cucumbers)," she said, "then I got in the car and went again. The truck was still there."

She went home, and suspecting something, checked the clock in the kitchen.

"It said 12:30 A.M.," Schwenk said. "That's when I realized I'd set my alarm on the new clock, but I hadn't set the time. I'd gotten up in the middle of the night."

Then she did what any true angler would have done. She set the clock, reset the alarm and got up at the real 5:00 A.M. to go fishing.

She laughed at herself as she told the story, and she flung the Woblure toward Cornucopia again.

"I got Frank Bartles at home," she said.

Frank Bartles?

"Yeah, I got him at home in the bedroom," she said. "You should come home and see my live-in man."

She was talking about a life-size poster of Bartles, half of the Bartles and Jaymes wine cooler duo. Schwenk and her sister had seen the standups at a liquor store and asked the store's manager if they could have the men.

"He said, 'If you girls can use those men, just take them,' " Schwenk said.

She and her sister cut the two men apart, and Bartles has been standing in her bedroom since.

"Some days Frank puts his foot down, and I can't go fishing," Schwenk said, and she cackled.

Most days, though, Bartles is understanding, and Schwenk fishes. She stands on her rock, soaks up Lake Superior's beauty and appreciates life.

"There's so much to be thankful for, and we take it all for granted," she said.

She casted and retrieved and remembered fish she'd caught on other days.

"You know, you get that feeling right there when you have one on," she said, touching her stomach with a gloved hand. And she sent the Woblure zinging toward Cornucopia.

Checkout Time

I suppose I'm looking for cheap thrills. I want cottony clouds and sunlit ore boats and the warm caress of a summer breeze.

What have we got? Off-lake winds with the bite of a thousand terriers, scudding skies that don't know whether to cry tears or spit bullets, and an inch of greasy thaw on the land.

The rest of the world is worried about global warming and we can't get back-to-back days over 45 degrees.

April.

I say box it up, mark it *Return to Sender* and carry it down to the post office.

I know. Out where things creep and unfold and bud, progress is being made. The naturalists tell me this. My friends report it to me. But I'm not convinced.

I saw my first butterfly the other day, but it was having trouble staying aloft. Still had its Sorels on. Six of 'em. HA HA HA HA!!!

I'm sick. I'll admit it. You can tell me all you want about your birds returning from the South and your pussy willows unfurling and your raccoons roving. I need more. Much more. Is it asking too much to sit down on a tussock of what looks to be dried grass and get up 10 minutes later without looking as if you should still be wearing diapers?

I'm tired of oozing topsoil and winter's debris caught in naked shrubs.

I'm tired of that patch of ice in the shady spot on my driveway that refuses to melt. Try to negotiate that remnant of the glacial epoch on trash day when you're lugging two 30-gallon garbage cans to the curb and a fluff of new snow has flocked the ice field. My neighbors must get up early just to catch the spectacle.

And I'm weary of cold.

The other day, I got my annual form-letter invitation to the governor's fishing opener festivities. The letter to the state's journalists opened like this: "With the early spring we're having this year . . ."

The letter came on a morning—an April morning—when the overnight low in Duluth was seven degrees. The wind chill was three below zero that day. And I'm supposed to be thinking about fishing with the governor? I'm too busy wondering about changing the oil in my snowblower again to speculate about what size jig head is likely to produce walleyes on opening day.

I tried to humor this season along for awhile. I kept my skis out. I retained my Northern "yeah-it's-tough-but-we-like-it-that-way" facade. But my patience with this insufferable condition is wearing thin.

And think how the gulls must feel. You want to see something pitiful? Go down to Canal Park in Duluth. Take a walk. If anything typifies the desperation of this stark page on the calendar, it is the Canal Park gulls.

Talk about frustration. Talk about crazed animals. Talk about birds on the down and out.

These are gulls gone bad.

Raised on french fries, popcorn and the slitted remains of portion-control ketchup packets, these birds have come back from the South on some biological timetable only to find their ecosystem shattered—no tourists.

No popcorn. Few fries. Token offerings of ketchup.

Watch them circle and taunt any sign of human life. They dip and dart like avian wolves moving in for a kill.

They're wild, deprived, hungry critters—caught in the cruel time warp between March and May.

Right here with the rest of us.

Summer

Well Worth It

We had been busy not catching lake trout for a couple
of hours. Just the two of us in the 14-foot boat, trolling
around Burntside Lake near Ely.

There are better places to catch lake trout. We knew
that. But on this day—the Sunday of fishing's opening
weekend—there were few places better for not catching
lake trout.

The day was warm. The breeze was soft. We had a
generous supply of bite-size Hershey bars.

But even dedicated anglers like the two of us can take
only so much success at not catching fish. After a couple
of hours we pulled up our lines.

On the way back to my buddy's cabin, we decided to
boat over to another friend's place on the lake. He'd

been walleye fishing the day before. We wanted a report.

He had seen us coming, and he caught our boat as it coasted up to his dock. His wife was there, too, and the three girls, and the black Lab and the new kitten.

What happened over the next 15 or 20 minutes was what makes summer and Northern Minnesota two of the best things ever to come together. To be honest, I didn't even think much about it until later. Then I realized what a wonderful few minutes we had enjoyed.

What we did was sit. And talk. And feel the sun. And look at the water. And listen to the lake caress the dock.

We talked about the previous day's walleye fishing and the current day's lake trout fishing. We talked about the new kitten and the black Labs.

We talked about fly-fishing for whitefish. We talked about how we had celebrated Mother's Day. We talked about plans for next weekend.

My buddy and I never left the boat, although the two Labradors who had been not fishing with us hopped out to stake tentative claims to this new territory. The kids hung around for a few minutes but soon figured their own pursuits were more interesting than our adult chatter.

So it was just the four of us. Our friend held the boat by the gunwale. His wife sat on the warm planks of the old dock. My buddy and I sat in the boat with our feet propped up, which put our chests and legs at the proper angle to accept the sun's warmth.

The air smelled like water and white pines. The boat rocked just enough to feel good. At one point two loons surfaced nearby, looked at the world and each other, thought about things for a second and submerged again.

It was, in short, the kind of day Northern Minnesotans dream about for much of November and December and January and February and March and April. Count 'em. Six months.

Then, almost suddenly, it is the middle of May and you are sitting in a boat with your fishing rods strung and the sun is baking you in your plaid wool shirt and the lake is blue and liquid again and you're talking about how the walleyes were biting yesterday.

We talked until all the talking that needed to be done was done. Then we loaded the dogs and fired up the outboard. Our friend shoved us off.

As we bounced back down the lake toward my buddy's cabin, I leaned back and looked at the clouds. They were puffy and white, and gilded at the edges by the sun behind them. They were the clouds you see in Minnesota in the summertime.

The motor purred. The hull slapped the waves. The islands slid past.

It is worth waiting for.

What's Tomorrow Mean?

The man and the girl were headed north. He was driving. She was checking out the world from her car seat. Their camping gear was in back.

It was just the two of them this time, dad and daughter. It just sort of turned out that way. Mom couldn't go. She had to work.

The girl was three and a half now, and she knew some things about camping. She knew that birch bark helped start fires. She knew that sometimes you got to pick blueberries for the pancakes. She knew she always wore a life jacket in the canoe.

A lot of things she didn't know, however, and she intended to get the answers on this drive north.

"Do worms have mouths?"

"Are we going to camp by Megan's house?"

"Deer and moose don't bite, do they?"

The questions carried the two of them north until they had pitched their tent on the shores of Divide Lake near Isabella. They had found the three-site campground where the map told them it was, and they had it all to themselves on a perfect day.

They ate lunch—peanut butter and jelly sandwiches, of course. They made Kool-Aid, but Dad had bought the kind that you have to mix with sugar. He had thought it was presweetened. He hadn't brought sugar.

"This tastes bad," the girl said.

She was right. They drank water.

After lunch, they tried a nap, but it didn't take. Oh, it took pretty well on Dad, but it didn't take hold on the little girl. She couldn't decide which foam pad to sleep on, and just where to put her stuffed Snoopy dog and the Pound Puppy, and whether she wanted her sleeping bag zipped or unzipped.

"Dad, I'm not sleepy," she said finally.

He believed her, and they went to gather firewood. Along the way, they talked.

"Are clouds air?"

"I'll bet the bears are taking a nap."

"I'll bet we hear some loon calls."

They got detoured in a tangle of blown-down balsam fir, and the little girl was suddenly in a different world.

"This is the Rocky Mountains," she said. "I have to go looking for animals, because I'm a forest creature."

And for the next 10 minutes, she might as well have been. She scaled balsam trunks, crawled under bushes and climbed over logjams. Dad sawed a chunk of downed spruce for firewood and watched her. He couldn't help but think that all of her climbing, all of her exploring, all of her little risk-taking would serve her well some day when she was off leading trips into the bush on her own.

After a while, Dad found himself doing more thinking than sawing. He thought 39 was a good age to be if you had a three-year-old to study. Her playing reminded him of good memories from his own childhood—the smell of damp ground, the feel of cool grass, the magic of tents and forts.

At the same time, he found himself thinking about his parents, imagining them sitting on some picnic table 35 years ago watching a skinny little boy scrabble in the dirt and transport himself to imaginary places. They must have enjoyed watching him the same way he enjoyed watching his daughter now. Funny, he had never expected to grow closer to his parents by sitting at a campsite in the boonies with his daughter.

Well, they split the firewood and they ate macaroni and cheese and they roasted marshmallows that night. They saw a pair of loons, a beaver and three mallards.

When it got dark, they crawled into the tent and their sleeping bags. They were talking about what they might do the next day when the little girl came up with one last question.

"What's tomorrow mean?"

"Tomorrow," Dad said, "means the day after today."

"Oh."

And as tomorrows go, Dad thought, it was going to be a good one.

Thunderbolts

We lay in the tent, waiting for the storm to find us. It was going to be a good one.

One moment the tent was dark. The next moment it was as if someone outside had unleashed a battery of searchlights on a sky of aluminum foil. Between the light shows, the clouds played bumper cars, and the rumbling of the collisions rolled off into infinity.

The thunder and lightning had been playing for almost an hour now, and still the wind and rain had held off. Only the humidity and the anticipation had built.

The three of us lay across the tent floor like little sausages, lined up on our sleeping bags, too warm to slide inside. One of us—the four-year-old—was snoozing, oblivious to the impending storm. The other two of us—the four-year-old's parents—lay there, our heads propped on stuff-sacks full of clothes.

We were camped on a rocky shoreline in the canoe country north of Ely. We'd been out for a couple of days.

"You going to try to go to sleep?" one of us said.

"Not yet," came the answer. "I think I'll wait for the storm."

Earlier that evening, sensing the front moving in, we had moved the tent farther from the roots of a white pine. We had heard the stories of lightning strikes that followed tree roots under a tent, killing or injuring campers sleeping inside.

It is hard to say just how far a white pine's roots might extend horizontally beneath the soil, but we felt better after moving the tent.

The wind was picking up now, coming out of the east, billowing the mosquito netting inward like a spinnaker sail at one end of the tent. Then the rain began to drill the tent fly, and we zipped the storm fly shut except for a small space at the top for ventilation.

The lightning was coming more often in bolts, the kind that began with a cannon blast and finished with a sound like thick canvas ripping at a seam. Silently, I counted the seconds between the lightning and its thunder.

One-thousand-one, one-thousand-two, one-thousand-three . . .

Eight seconds total. Five seconds to a mile. The storm was still a mile and a half away.

Rain pelted the tent fly, but we weren't worried about getting wet. The tent had shed a lot of rain in its time. It was a good tent.

Another bolt of white. Another bumping of boxcars on the railroad tracks. The storm was getting closer.

We lay there in silence, contemplating our mortality, figuring out odds. You don't honestly think you're going to die in a thunderstorm. You figure your odds of living, of waking up in your sleeping bag and having some pancakes the next morning, are pretty good. That's what your logical mind thinks.

On the other hand, your odds aren't nearly as good as they would be if you were driving down the road in your car or sitting in your home. You are, after all, lying on the wet forest floor somewhere in the vicinity of a few mature white pines, atop a hunk of rock.

Another ripping of the atmosphere, and every detail of the tent was illuminated. Then the attendant clap of thunder. We were still in the heart of the storm.

You can't help wondering what it would be like, going this way. One second you'd be lying there, concerned but comfortable with the two people you love most in the world. A second later—that would be it. Would it feel hot? Would it feel at all?

You think about that, and you squeeze your wife's hand a little bit, and it squeezes back, and you lie there and think some more.

You think about the way you live life. About the situations you put yourself and some vulnerable four-year-old into. You think about taking risks, and the value in that.

You wouldn't do it differently. You know that.

But that doesn't mean you can't lie there, awake, waiting to find out if you'll wake up in the morning.

Some time later, the rain let up. The gaps between the lightning and the thunder began to grow longer again.

"Good-night," she said.

"Good-night," I said.

In the morning, we ate pancakes.

Benny

If you close your eyes, you can see him. The face grizzled with whiskers. The glasses beginning their slide down his nose. The camouflage jacket with puffs of down escaping from the rip in his sleeve.

He would have been steadying a cup of coffee on his knee at Jim's Bait. Or casting from a shelf of ice into Lake Superior. Or tending a campfire at a backcountry campsite on a brook trout lake.

His name was Benny Larson. He was a fisherman.

Benny died at 54, a victim of cancer.

His exploits with rod and reel were the stuff of quiet legend among those who know the North Shore and the Gunflint Trail north of Grand Marais.

Benny caught many brook trout of more than five pounds and one of more than six—rare feats here in

Minnesota waters. In one remarkable day, he caught three lake trout that weighed 14, 28 and 31 pounds. He helped Helen Kessling, then a 78-year-old Gunflint Trail summer resident, catch a 33 1/2-pound lake trout on Clearwater Lake north of Grand Marais.

That all of this happened in Benny's shortened life comes as no surprise to those who knew him.

"Benny fishes four hundred days a year, you know," Jim Keuten, owner of Jim's Bait, once said.

"He was really a hard-core fisherman," said Benny's longtime friend Bill Houle of Cloquet. "He was the type of person who never gave up. He always felt the fish were there."

Benny grew up in Duluth and began making trips to the Gunflint Trail with a friend of the family. He fell in love with the country.

He worked various jobs in Duluth and in 1976 began working for Jim's Bait, where he became a fixture of sorts. He worked at Jim's for about six years before he bought a wholesale bait distributorship from Keuten.

From 1982 until his death, Benny ran a route in his 1978 Datsun pickup, serving about 25 bait outlets along the North Shore and up the Gunflint Trail. He lived in a modest cabin on Aspen Lake north of Grand Marais.

Though not a loner in any sense of the word, Benny lived by himself most of his life. He was married only briefly and had no children.

In an interview a few days before his death, Benny laughingly challenged Keuten's assessment of his fishing frequency. It wasn't close to four hundred days a year, Benny said.

"But I probably got a good two hundred in," he said. "Especially when I was working at the bait shop. It gets your fever up."

Brook trout fishing was always Benny's specialty. He fished for everything—walleyes, lake trout, rainbows, steelhead. But his first love was brookies.

His friend Bill Houle was there the day Benny caught his six-pound-plus brook trout. It was in the mid-1960s. Keep in mind, the current Minnesota brook trout record, set in 1967, is six pounds, two ounces.

Benny caught the fish on a Prescott spinner, he said. He weighed it only on a pocket De-Liar scale.

"It was over six," House said. "I think it was about 6 3/4 or 6 1/2. I said, 'That could be close to the state record.' He said, 'It very well could be, but it's more important to return it to the water.' "

Which is exactly what he did. Benny returned most of his big brook trout to the water, Houle said. He had a respect bordering on reverence for the species.

"It's like fishing for jewels," Benny said.

He wasn't above eating a few of those jewels. Kessling, the Gunflint Trail cabin owner who was a friend of Benny's for 35 years, recalled a memorable day of brookie fishing with him. Kessling, now 80, and Benny had portaged into a canoe-country brook trout lake a few years ago.

"I was casting, and I had caught an almost four-pound brook trout," Kessling said from her home in Chicago. "Then Benny got a hit. He was using a bobber. The line broke up by his rod tip. I cast out and got his bobber with my hook—and he got a four-pound brook trout, too.

"We had 22 pounds of brook trout to carry out of there. We each got our limit."

That was the same kind of luck Benny was having the day he caught his three big lake trout in 1968. Ironically, he was trying to get to a brook trout lake that day. He decided he might as well troll for lake trout while he was crossing Clearwater Lake, just off the Gunflint Trail north of Grand Marais.

"I was using a T-55 silver Flatfish," Benny said. "I got the first fish (a 14-pounder) and took it back. I started over and got the second one (a 26-pounder). Then I got the third one.

"I never did go brook trout fishing that day."

Benny was not only an excellent fisherman. He was an innovator of fishing techniques.

He pioneered, at least on the North Shore, the use of long rods and light lines, said Duluth outdoors writer Michael Furtman. Benny was among the first to fish through Lake superior's ice for Kamloops rainbow trout, said Duluth photographer and fisherman Larry Alvar. Benny also invented fishing lures, most notably the Norwegian Wart and the Benny Bug.

He created the Norwegian Wart, a walleye ice-fishing spoon, 12 or 15 years ago, Keuten said, and they are still sold at Jim's Bait. Benny told Keuten he settled on that name because "there's already a Swedish Pimple."

The Benny Bug was never marketed commercially, but many North Shore rainbow trout anglers use it for Kamloops rainbow trout.

"It's very tantalizing," said Alvar. " 'Loopers are persnickety. There are times when the Benny Bug is the only thing they'll come in and munch on."

Benny was a dedicated tinkerer who could make or repair almost anything, friends said.

"He could take people's garbage and make functional things," Furtman said. "He'd take old bulk (fishing line) spools from the bait shop and make water filters out of them."

He had a distinctive style of tinkering.

"He wasn't Mr. Neat," Keuten said. "When Benny got done with a job, it looked like the landing of the Normandy invasion."

Appearances were never a major concern for Benny. He wore work pants and work shirts, fishing caps that looked like they'd been fishing, and—for years—the old camouflage jacket.

"He must have worn it for 15 years," Houle said.

Benny finally retired that jacket with fanfare.

"We burned it," Benny said. "We had a ceremony."

It wasn't the size of Benny's wardrobe people remember as much as the size of his heart.

He would help hapless campers he met on the trail. He was caretaker and friend to Kessling. He would willingly share any fishing information with customers at Jim's—except for his secret brook trout spots.

Furtman recalled the time Benny patched a canoeist's punctured canoe with spruce gum. Alvar said it was Benny who taught him to safely walk on Lake Superior's jumbled ice.

But perhaps a story told by Kessling, Benny's Gunflint Trail friend, best illustrates the Benny many knew.

Kessling was having a problem with mice at her summer cabin, but she didn't want to hurt them.

"I couldn't see killing them," Kessling said. "The trapping—that upset me. So Benny took his minnow trap and set it up under the porch."

The mice would crawl into the trap and be unable to find their way out, but they'd remain alive.

"In the morning, when we had caught four or five, we'd drive the mice to the dump and release them," Kessling said. "Benny would talk to them. He'd say, 'Now, don't come back.'

"I tell you the truth. There is nobody like Benny."

Gooseberry Delights

One of the fringe benefits of being a trout fisherman is that it requires you to wear waders, and one of the fringe benefits of putting on waders is that the act requires you to sit down.

Most often the places where you sit down to change into your waders are beautiful, or at the least quiet and green and near the sound of moving water.

I was thinking about that as I eased down onto a beach of pebbles and driftwood at the mouth of the Gooseberry River. Sitting on the rocks, I kicked off my hiking boots and slithered into my waders.

In one direction, I looked upstream and saw the river come snaking down from the hills, making one final lazy bend before reaching the lake. I looked over my shoulder and watched Lake Superior come lapping around a knoll of rock into the bay at the river's mouth.

I took my time getting into my waders. I was in no hurry, and this was a good place not to be hurrying.

I had set aside the afternoon for some ambling. Some poking around. Some aimless exploring.

To be honest about it, fishing hadn't been on the agenda. I had come to Gooseberry Falls State Park on the shore mostly to take some pictures of wild flowers and to soak up the splendor of this day. Any place along the Shore—or inland—would have been fine, but I knew that Paul Sundberg, the park manager at Gooseberry, would have some good patches of wildflowers staked out.

Sundberg led me along the Gitchi Gummi trail toward a rock clematis that a visitor had told him about.

I wouldn't have known a clematis from a columbine, but Sundberg did, and we found it right where it was supposed to be, twining its way among some birches on a west-facing hillside. Its flowers were lavender and showy. My plant book said that Charles Darwin, when studying a close relative of this twining plant, found that "each new leafstalk revolves as it grows, making a full circle every five or six hours until it finds a solid object to climb."

We upright mammals go about our hurried lives, and there on some hillside, a clematis is revolving along, looking for something solid to hang onto.

After Sundberg left me, I moved along other trails, past marsh marigolds, bluebells, strawberry plants, purple violets and yellow violets.

Gooseberry was a profusion of life. The ferns were unfurling. The white-throated sparrows were hitting all the high notes. A veery sounded like he was whistling as he fell down a drainspout. A self-conscious ruffed grouse tried to drum up a mate.

Early June is a happening time of year.

There is no time for hesitation. If you are a wild thing in the North in June, you mate or flower or nest or unfurl or pollinate. You don't wait around.

If you're a chorus frog and it means you chorus all night, you do it. If you're a grouse and it means you pound your wings on your chest every four minutes around the clock, you do it. If you're a clematis and it means you spiral your way through the woods seeking support, you do it.

And if you're a fly fisherman, you don't pass up the opportunity to fool a trout.

I tied on a streamer fly, the name of which I do not know, and waded into Lake Superior where the Gooseberry ends its run. I was alone in this fine piece of country, alone with my thoughts about this season of fullness, alone at the edge of the most expansive lake in the world, tossing a creation of feathers and flash that was supposed to look like a minnow.

It must have. It fooled a tiny rainbow trout, one that the Department of Natural Resources had stocked only days or hours before. He was smaller than regulations permit keeping, and I wouldn't have kept him anyway. But even at eight inches, he was wild with fight and determination. I admired his spunk and told him so.

I plucked a few more of the tiny fish from the lake and put them back before I had had enough, and then I went back to the gravel bar to slip out of my waders.

If I had been in no hurry before, I was even more content now to let the wader transition linger. The lake had been cold, and the sun felt good on my jeans. The smooth stones were warm under my hands.

I sat there, soaking up some of that same light and heat that was making the country come alive around me.

It is a fine and rewarding thing to be a fisher of trout. And sometimes the fishing has little to do with the trout themselves.

No Name Falls

On the topographic maps the location just ahead of us was nameless. Just a couple of hash marks across the meandering blue path of the Gods River. Merely a set of rapids, according to the map.

But we had hugged the right shoreline just in case the map might have underestimated the rapids. Good thing.

We could hear the roar of the water long before we reached the drop, and we could see the spray over the river glistening in the horizontal rays of the evening sun.

One by one, we pulled over in our four canoes, and we got out to assess what turned out to be not merely rapids but significant waterfalls.

The eight of us were eleven days into a three-week

odyssey that would deliver us to Hudson's Bay in northern Manitoba. We had chosen the Gods River for its primitive beauty—clear water, quick current and challenging but manageable white water. Already it had delivered all that it had promised.

We also knew the river held brook trout. Fishing wasn't the primary reason we had made this trip, but we were hoping to catch brookies wherever we could.

This spot—we dubbed it No Name Falls—was supposed to be full of brook trout. Each summer on the Gods River, anglers using barbless hooks and heavy spinners take many brook trout in the four- and five-pound class, some even larger.

We Minnesotans struggle to catch one-pounders from our streams back home.

A couple of us had tried to catch some brookies upstream on the Gods, but without success. We were eager to cast into the froth below this set of falls.

We made camp along the portage trail that skirted the falls. It was already 7:30 P.M., but the days are long in northern Manitoba in the summer and we had plenty of daylight left.

Jim and Peg threw together a macaroni and cheese dinner. They cooked over a small fire nestled among granite outcroppings at the edge of the river.

That a falls of this magnitude would not bear a name on the map amazed us. We had come upon a thick tongue of water thrusting itself from the river above into a maelstrom below.

The Gods River is two or three hundred yards wide in places, but here it condensed its volume into a single chute not more than 30 yards wide. The drop itself was not more than eight or 10 feet, but the power of the current, squeezed through that neck of rock, created a series of huge standing waves. The river had carved itself a pool in the rock below. The fastest water shot through the middle of the pool, and eddies along both sides sent strong currents back upstream.

So swift was the water in the eddies that anyone who slipped into the river would be swept almost instantly into the main current at the base of the falls. Nobody wanted to think about what would happen after that.

Ken, our leader, suggested safety precautions. We would fish from a long, sloping rock at the edge of the falls only if somebody else were present. And always there would be a throw-line nearby in case someone did go in.

Standing on that warm shoulder of granite, with Phyllis looking on, I snapped an orange spoon to the swivel at the end of my fishing line. The barbs of the hook were pinched down in accordance with the regulations for this stretch of river. I tossed the spoon into the fastest water and retrieved it until it hit the eddy line. I let the eddy carry it upstream, flirting with the fast water.

I made a few casts. I made another. As I retrieved I could see the spoon twisting in that emerald water. Then I saw the brook trout.

I don't know how many. Three. Four, maybe. Could have been five. Each of them as long as a forearm. They were all coming for the spoon.

One of them got it, the others vanished and the fight was on.

All river fish seem to fight better than their counterparts in flat waters, and this one was no exception. Part of that power must have been a result of the way the fish used the current to its advantage. It didn't matter. I was fast to the strongest brookie I'd ever encountered.

I don't remember the fight lasting long. I remember the brookie's dance atop that churning water. I remember seeing it flop and splash, but I don't recall hearing the struggle. The surging of the falls drowned out all of that.

And then I was guiding the fish into a crevice in the rock where we felt we could land it without risking a swim. I gave Phyllis my rod and pounced on the fish with both hands. It was not big by Gods River standards—two pounds, maybe. But it was all brookie, resplendent with red speckles on its sides, the characteristic wormy pattern across its broad back, and fins the color of a sunset. We decided we would keep it for breakfast.

I had not finished cleaning it before Phyllis had her first one on. She played it, landed it and held it up in the evening's amber light. It was a good three pounds and a male, judging by its color. Its belly was a brilliant shade of tangerine and its fins far richer in color than the female's. Brookies spawn in the fall, and late July was not too soon for the males to begin taking on their spawning hues.

Phyllis let the sunset light play on the fish for a few moments. I remember reading once in Aldo Leopold's *A Sand County Almanac* about a man who had not believed in God until he discovered warblers—their numbers, their beauty, the wonder of their migrations. I have spent many Sundays far from a church, but when I looked at the brook trout my wife held that night on the Gods River, I had no doubt that some power far beyond mere humans was in charge of the universe.

The fishing slowed, and night slipped over northern Manitoba. We put away the rods, but I knew then my trip on the Gods was complete.

Around a small fire, we sipped blackberry tea and waited to see if the northern lights would make an appearance. This was the first night of the trip that mosquitoes were not a serious factor. The air was cool, and the fire felt good.

It must have been almost midnight when someone looked up and saw the lights. We moved away from the fire to the big lump of granite and lay down to enjoy the show. The green lights shimmered across the sky. They pulsated and wavered, receded and rose again. It was a wild, spell-binding performance made even more powerful by the river racing by with its unbridled energy.

Somewhere beneath it all, in the tumble of currents below No Name Falls, swam some marvelous speckled creatures.

Fall

Saying Grace

I'm not much at saying grace. Although I grew up going to Sunday School almost every week, and today carry with me a clear sense of a greater power, in my childhood home we simply sat down and ate.

Now, though, in my adult home, we say grace at almost every meal. While it's an appropriate thing to do, I'll admit I feel a little empty about it much of the time.

I think I know why.

The reason came to me the other night when we sat down to eat some pheasant and grouse and woodcock and wild rice. It wasn't a fancy meal. Fancy meals are hard to come by in our kitchen, where an eight-month-old hangs suspended in a sling seat on one side of the table, gumming a soft plastic pretzel and drooling.

Still, it was going to be a nice meal.

As eager as I was to sample the wild fare before us, I felt it especially important to have a few words with the Great Spirit before we began.

I realized I had some strong feelings about that food on the table. I had shot the pheasants and the grouse and some of the woodcock. I had taken lives, and now I was fortifying my own with the result of those deaths.

The rice had been a gift from some acquaintances, and although I hadn't harvested it, I knew whose hands had. That, too, seemed to require acknowledgment.

So I said a few brief words about sky and land and water and wild things. My message wasn't eloquent, but it felt right.

That meal made me realize how few times I feel that kind of connection with the food I eat.

We have removed ourselves, almost entirely, from the process of growing or gathering or raising or hunting our food. A man brings a pizza to the door. We pop a compartmentalized dinner in the microwave. We buzz the drive-through and munch fries at traffic lights.

Not many of us, any more, kill chickens on the stump out back or gather eggs from under hens or butcher hogs in the barnyard.

I don't mean to equate hunting, as most of us do it today, with raising livestock. But hunting does afford an opportunity, increasingly rare, to be personally involved with the food that ends up on our tables.

I feel different when I'm eating something I've hunted or gathered than when I'm pulling fries from a sack. My wild food is not simply a bird on a plate; it is part of the country from which it came. The pheasant is part of the sloughs or the prairie grasses or the willow thickets. The woodcock is part of the alder bottoms or the young aspen and the North from which it came. The mallards are part of the cattail marsh and the pondweed and the wild rice.

When I eat pheasant, I see corn stubble and black soil and remember weary legs. When I eat a duck, I smell the marsh and remember being cold. When I eat grouse, I am part of a sunny October hillside, listening to the aspen leaves rustle.

I feel a responsibility for the lives I have taken. Taking a creature's life is not a frivolous act. Many of us who hunt pay our respects, silently, at the moment of the kill. Beyond that, we owe it to the animal to see that it is used wisely and completely.

I like to prepare the game I bring home. I bang around in a warm kitchen, browning meat, boiling and soaking rice. Or I sit on the back porch letting the sweet smoke from a charcoal fire waft past me, carrying the scent of a pheasant on the grill.

To me, that is all a part of the process of hunting and gathering—a continuing participation with the game until it is on the table.

I can see something similar happening with my wife and daughter, who together plant carrot seeds each spring, thin the plants in July and pull up carrots in October. They know those plants. They have spent time with them. My daughter loves the taste of our garden carrots, and I think part of the reason is that her little fingers have grubbed around in the dirt with them.

My regret is that these connections with the earth and its creatures are so rare.

We still say grace over the pizza that comes to the door. But for me, it isn't the same.

Black Brule

Full darkness had come, and it was time to get on down the river.

We picked up our fly rods, doused the lantern and picked our way to the canoe. A whippoorwill was calling in the woods.

It was just the two of us old friends and another old friend—Wisconsin's Brule River. We had come this night, in September, because we knew fall would deepen soon and the evenings would inspire thoughts of woodstoves and deer shacks instead of canoes and brown trout.

We had come over from the city as soon as we could break away. We had found the river, as always, narrow and quiet and inviting at Stone's Bridge. We had paddled a couple of miles before stopping for supper. Now, bellies full and eyes adjusting to the darkness, we pushed away from the simple dock.

Never had I been on the Brule in such total blackness. An afternoon rain had given way to a drippy evening. The cloud cover had been complete at twilight. Out on the main channel of the river, the pines and cedars were charcoal shapes against a sky of soot. The mist, thick enough to feel on hands and cheeks, further blurred the visible edges of the river.

I know the Brule from only a few years of visits, most of them by day. My friend knows the river as only one can who has been paddling and poling it since a childhood of idyllic summers here. I wondered, paddling bow, how many times he had spent nights this dark on the river.

"Cast to the right now," he said. "About one o'clock."

I sent the Hank's Creation, a thimble-sized surface popper, into a colorless void.

We moved down the river, through all the old place names: May's Rips, the Dining Room Pool, Cedar Island, the Willow Pool and Sally's. My friend knows the names. In most cases, I know only the places.

This is still new to me, this night fly-casting, this committing the canoe to the loud sucking of rapids, this navigating by sentinel pines against murky backdrops.

I bungled casts. I spooked trout. I put my Hank's into leaning cedars.

As unrefined as I am at the game, I am willing to keep missing strikes and reading the river until I have mastered this experience. It is too good not to get better at it.

The Brule offers far more than the hope of hooking up with a brown trout. Between pools, we listened to barred owls tuning up for the night's symphony. We stopped casting when the coyotes began to yap and whine. We wondered in silence at invisible splashes, slurps and murmurs.

We spoke some, when speech seemed necessary, and we did it in a hush that came naturally. The river seemed to belong to the owls and the coyotes and the deer. There was no need for a couple of humans to come muddying the night with chatty conversation.

I'm not sure what a spiritual experience is. But I know that on the Brule, at night, with a fly rod in my hand and wonder in my soul, I feel a sense of spirit that I have known in few other places. And it has less to do with the fly rod than the wonder.

At a streamside dock below Cedar Island, we unfolded stiff legs and changed places in the canoe. We moved on downriver. My friend sliced the heavy air with purposeful casts and smooth retrieves. I studied the efficiency of his motions as closely as one can study someone casting a black fly rod against a smudge of shoreline on a starless night.

It was after midnight when we pulled up to the dock at my friend's cabin. Sleep came quickly and morning even more quickly.

Before we headed back to the city, we grabbed a couple of oranges and went down to the river. Not that we had anything more to do there. The canoe had been pulled up the night before. The paddles were put away. But we stood there just the same, looking and listening and thinking.

It seemed only right. When a river has given you that much, you don't leave without saying goodbye.

Minnesota Oysters

From a distance, it was difficult to determine what was in the plastic bag that was sitting on the work bench.

Whatever was in there, there were several of them. Maybe a dozen. Each was the size of a large egg. They looked to be soft and moist.

Tom Engel, Department of Natural Resources forest wildlife coordinator, pulled one of the elliptical objects from the bag.

"Moose oysters," Engel said. "Want to try one?"

This was Monday noon, three days into Minnesota's 1989 moose season. Engel had spent the morning registering moose for happy hunters at the Tofte registration station.

While measuring antlers, tagging chunks of moose

meat and getting other pertinent information, Engel would ask the hunters—if they had shot a bull—"Did you bring me the oysters?"

They'd smile, then dig out an Almond Joy candy bar bag or some such container with a pair of the gray goose eggs inside. Engel would add the pair to his growing collection.

Now it was lunchtime, and Engel was ready to prepare one of his culinary specialties—deep-fried moose oysters.

OK. Enough double-talk. Moose oysters are the items a bull moose requires two of if he hopes to perform his role in perpetuating his species.

Yep.

Testicles.

Engel had already carved a lump of butter into a cast-iron skillet that had been warming atop a two-burner Coleman stove.

While the butter started to bubble, Engel slit the skin casings on a couple of oysters. He then peeled all of the skin from each one. The process was something like removing the skin from a bratwurst. Maybe easier.

Inside was more soft gray matter. Sort of pulpy looking. About the texture of an eyeball.

The butter was reaching the right temperature now. Engel worked quickly. He sliced the gray matter into discs, the way someone would slice a zucchini. Then Engel patted each slice in a bowl of Fryin' Magic breading. One by one, he tossed 13 breaded discs into the hot butter.

Engel said he tried the moose oysters initially when he worked his first moose registration in this same garage in 1983. He'd heard about people eating Rocky Mountain oysters—the equivalent body parts of sheep or hogs or calves—and decided the moose parts were worth a try.

Bill Peterson, DNR wildlife manager at Grand Marais, and his wife, Dale, always put on a party the first Saturday night of the season at Tofte. That was where Engel sizzled his first batch of moose oysters. They were a hit.

Engel flipped each disc and let it sizzle on the second side for a couple more minutes. Finally the batch was finished. Engel removed the skillet from the heat and spatulaed each golden goodie onto a paper plate.

"Help yourself," he said.

I had a perfectly good turkey sandwich in my own sack lunch. I had an apple. I had already sampled some of Dale Peterson's leftover moose tenderloin, which was excellent.

Which is to say, I wasn't starving.

Ah, what the heck, I figured. I grabbed one of the delicate discs and popped it into my mouth. I began chewing.

Have you ever had fricasseed lymph gland? I haven't either, but I decided the sensation would have been about the same.

But you know what?

The darn thing was good. It was mostly Fryin' Magic and squish, but it was a firm squish. I had two more, and I wasn't just being polite.

About that time, another group of hunters pulled up outside to register a moose. Engel wiped his hands and headed for the door.

When he got outside, he saw the moose. It was a bull.

I'm not sure, but I think I saw Engel smile.

Nett Gain

The river was boiling with ducks. Even in the morning half-light, you could see they were ring-necked ducks, nearly all of them.

As the canoes moved along, the fleet of ducks would swim ahead, creating a grid of intersecting wakes on the water. Then the ducks would patter across the surface and take wing into the gray east.

Sooner or later, they would come back. They came at us in singles and pairs, low over the water, until they caught sight of the movement of our paddles. They would flare then, climbing fast, but you could see the whites of their bellies and the splotch of light color on their bills.

Gene Goodsky had known it would be this way. It nearly always is this way in October, at sunrise, on the

Nett River. The river is the outflow of Nett Lake, near Orr, where Goodsky and his Chippewa people have lived and hunted ducks for many decades.

Another ringbill—as these ducks are called—winged past, just over our heads. Goodsky, a member of the Bois Forte band of Lake Superior Chippewa, smiled.

We had come to watch and hunt ducks. We would take them from blinds, with shotguns, at the river's source on the rice-choked shores of Nett Lake.

The four of us—Duluth's Bob Hedburg, Ely's Bob Cary, Goodsky and myself—nearly had reached the blinds when a bald eagle took flight from across the river.

For Goodsky, it was like seeing an old friend. "There's the eagle. He's the one that takes care of all the cripples."

Goodsky was talking about wounded ducks that cannot be retrieved by hunters. If you were an eagle, Nett Lake would be a good place to live in October. The sprawling rice lake draws large numbers of ringbills, mallards and bluebills each fall. And the ducks draw duck hunters.

Although the lake is entirely within the Bois Forte Indian Reservation, non-Indian hunters may hunt there with guides from the reservation. Guiding duck hunters is a longstanding tradition in the seven-hundred-resident village of Nett Lake. On a weekend day in October, as many as 15 or 20 guides might be on the lake with hunting parties. Under band rules, each guide may take up to three hunters.

Now Goodsky had tossed a dozen bluebill decoys along the river's edge. The four of us were waiting in the grasses or behind the brushy blinds the Indians leave standing throughout the season. Goodsky and

Hedburg would do most of the early shooting. Cary tooted cleverly into a duck call, making mallard and diving-duck music come out the other end.

There was no urgency to this hunt. We had set up in the coming day's light, not in the vestiges of the waning night. Ducks had buzzed our decoys before the guns were out of their cases, but no one hustled for cover or lamented a missed opportunity.

There was a sense that the ducks would keep flying, and that they would be as cooperative as the hunt required. The mood was nurtured by Goodsky, who watched casually as we readied ourselves. He did not suggest any specific pattern or plan to our setup. It did not seem to matter to him that we already had passed up some shots. He was content to watch the lake and the sky and the comings and goings of ducks.

"Look there," he said. Another batch of ringbills—30 or 40 birds—lifted out of the rice and became black wings and necks against the sun. He stood in knee-high rubber boots, wearing jeans, a camouflage hooded sweatshirt and a tan Jones cap, waiting and watching.

He is accustomed to the movements of ducks on the lake. It is something not only to watch, but to listen to, Goodsky said. Often at this time of year he hears the big rafts of ringbills and bluebills rearranging themselves far out on the lake early in the morning. He likes it. "It sounds like boiling water."

The birds working the river were singles or pairs. One came in low, and Hedburg was ready. His 12-gauge Remington barked once. The duck tumbled into the river. Hedburg's Labrador retriever, Tobie, leaped into the water. In a few moments, he came snuffling back with a mouthful of drake ringbill.

What happened over the next several minutes might

be commonplace at Nett Lake, but it was the kind of hunt most of us dream about when we are lying on a sofa with a dog curled up nearby.

Cary quacked and purred into the duck call. Nobody ever sounded more like a mallard full of wild rice or a diving duck full of contentment. The ringbills kept coming off the lake to inspect the decoys. When we chose to shoot, the shots were tough to miss. Tobie brought eight ringbills back to the blind.

We could have taken another one and been finished for the day. With Cary choosing not to hunt, our limit was nine birds total—three apiece—but we saved one for another spot Goodsky wanted to show us out on the lake.

As we paddled through the rice on the main lake, Goodsky talked about other days and other hunts. He pointed to places where guides often take hunters—down by a creek mouth, off a point of ash trees, in some rushes. He spoke often of the late October and early November hunts, the kind that came with sleet and waves and ducks riding northwest winds. "That's when those big northern mallards come down. And northern bluebills. Right around the latter part of October, when you get colder days and colder nights."

We talked and ate sandwiches and drank coffee. The day was one of those windless October classics, when the sky and water are a deep blue, and the shorelines are brushed gold with tamaracks getting ready to shed needles.

Off in the distance, out beyond Spirit Island and its old Indian etchings in the rock, you could hear water boiling. There must have been hundreds, maybe a couple thousand, ducks out there.

We shot one more ringbill to complete our morning,

then paddled back down the river to our landing. We drifted past duck feathers and tamarack needles floating on the water. Then Cary and Hedburg saw something white drifting ahead of us. It appeared to be a feather from a bald eagle.

"You want it, Gene?" Cary asked.

"Sure," Goodsky said.

Eagle feathers are powerful symbols to Indians. I once asked an old Indian woman about the significance of such feathers, which you often see hanging near the doors of traditional Indian homes. She said, in so many Ojibwe words, that she couldn't share the meaning with me.

Cary handed the feather to Goodsky. He turned it slowly between his thumb and forefinger. Then he pulled a small red package from his shirt pocket. I thought maybe he was going to put the feather in the package, but instead he opened it, took out a pinch of loose tobacco and sprinkled it on the water. When he was through, he put the feather and the tobacco back in his pocket.

"Whenever we get something," he explained, "we give something back."

Finding the eagle feather, Goodsky said, had been more than coincidence. "I always figure that means we did something right."

Which was a nice feeling to take with us, paddling on down the river to the landing.

Heavenly Pothole

We had a good-looking spread, as duck hunters like to say.

Which meant that our decoys, two or three dozen of them, were bobbing at anchor just the way they are supposed to. They looked good, strung out on one side of our blind, with a nice pod of them on the other side. We'd thrown in three Canada geese just for effect.

Our canoe was tucked into the cattails, our camouflage netting was draped surreptitiously, our guns were loaded.

But do you think we could get a duck to come within a hundred yards of our hideaway?

Not a chance.

Every single, every pair, every flock we saw would scream by, hell-bent for someplace just north of us.

"There's a little pothole over there," my partner said. "They must like to go in there."

Like to? It was as if there were a magnet the size of a football field in that pothole and every duck had an iron plate in its belly.

Why is it that nearly every time you set up to hunt ducks this happens? There's always someplace "just over the ridge" that ducks love to go. You never see these places. You just know they're there. Someone saw one on the map. Or told you about it. Or you just watch the ducks long enough and become convinced of it.

This magic place is most often "a little pothole." It could just as easily be a big lake or a bog pond or a flooded field of corn. But it's always out of sight. And the ducks love it.

It's one thing to have a bunch of ducks swing by and look you over hard while they make three passes over your decoys. You might spook them with a soprano duck call or by showing them a bright patch of your cheek or by reaching out to grab your gun. But at least you had the chance to work them a little.

It's something else when they fly by at cruising altitude, never giving you so much as a blink.

They don't want anything to do with you. They want the little pothole just over the ridge.

But it won't be that way up in The Great Beyond. Nope.

You show up at the Pearly Gates dressed in waders patched heavily and still leaking. You're wearing a camouflage coat, a beat-up camo cap with fuzzy earflaps and gloves bearing the telltale tracks of many nose-wipings in the marsh. You're carrying a couple of bags of decoys, some of them rattling with shot. Your 12-gauge is in a case with a broken zipper.

"Duck hunter, eh?" St. Peter says.

"Yep."

"Take the first right," he says. "Watch the greasy clay on the side of the hill. And stay to the left side at the big puddle. It's deep on the right. Keep going a ways. Just over the next ridge, you'll come to a little pothole. Set up there."

Sure enough, there it is. It's the little pothole of your dreams. And sitting on it, dabbling wild rice in the shallows, is every duck that ever flew over your blind at warp speed in your first life.

There's a blind waiting for you. You notice something different about it: It's dry.

There's a black Labrador sitting there. He, too, has been waiting. The tag on his collar says his name is Zeke. He gives you a lick on the chin as you slide onto the sitting bench and dig out some shells.

You notice something else now. The patches and holes on your waders have healed shut. Your feet are warm. There's an old but serviceable kerosene heater in the blind. You fire it up. It feels good.

The ducks—mallards, mostly, but some pintails and woodies, too—that left the pothole when you walked out to the blind are starting to come back now.

Just look at them coming in. They want to be here. No tentative circling. None of this last-minute flaring. It's as if your blind is at the bottom of a giant funnel.

All of your old buddies are there too. Their waders have healed shut, too. The coffee in the thermoses is still warm, and Zeke always shakes off outside the blind after a retrieve.

Believe it.

That's how it will be, someday, in the little pothole just over the ridge.

Nature Tells Us

A heaviness lies upon the land, and the best the sky can muster is a thin gray. The color of November.

Comes now the season of enduring, of waiting, of girding up.

Walk around. All of the signs are in place.

The board at the tourist boat dock on the harbor reads: "Next Excursion—May 13." The evergreens in the median strips are burlapped against the press of winter's snow. Flocks of Bohemian waxwings, fresh into town from the northwest, swirl from mountain ash to birch and back to mountain ash.

There's a sense of finality, of quiet anticipation and preparation in the air. We do not go lightly into this dark season, whether we be humans or meadow mice.

The tansies, those yellow, button-topped wildflowers

of roadsides and vacant lots, now stand lean and dry and brown. The goldenrod is no longer golden, but withered and stiff and the color of old train cars. The cattails, once slim and neat, are now puffing their brown heads, dropping next year's seeds, making a mess. It looks like stuffing coming out of old furniture.

Just in time, the mice figure. They need the cattail puffings to line their nests. It is not uncommon, this arrangement between plant and animal.

Oak trees and gray squirrels have come to an understanding regarding acorns.

Mountain ash trees and Bohemian waxwings have reached an agreement about the tree's berries.

All of them—the mice and the birds and the trees—are getting ready for what's to come.

Some critters will leave. The eagles and the broadwings and the warblers—they are moving on.

More than 260,000 little birds already have winged along the North Shore this fall, heading south. At least 60,000 of the big birds—the ones that eat the little birds—have drifted over Hawk Ridge.

Gone to Iowa and Oklahoma and Louisiana for easy pickings.

The geese, too, are cleaving the sky with their great wings, rotating the point position in their "V" formations to make the going easier. Geese don't move unless it's time.

It's time.

All the signs say it's so. The streams are shrunken trickles, picking their way through exposed streambeds. The bear droppings, so fresh in September, have been pelted by cold rains, which have sent streaks the color of black raspberries running down the paths.

On the pond, skim ice reaches across, not quite sure enough of itself to cover the whole surface. It leaves just enough room to welcome a hen mallard, and she drops in, talking about what she's seen farther north.

Ice is of little concern to her. If the night is cold and still and the ice reaches too far by morning, she will simply leave.

Those of us who stay behind are left to make our stand. We put the mitten basket where we can get at it. We keep a coat on the hook in the hall. We hunch our shoulders to the wind, and we pull our collars close and we watch the sky.

Like the mice, the geese and the waxwings, we know what's coming.

Winter

Good Ice

The ice came fast. It came on cold, windless days and on colder, windless nights.

It glazed the North Country lakes, and then it thickened. A week. Two weeks. Three.

Chel Anderson of Tofte was there. Out there, alone or with others, on the lakes or on the Poplar River—skating. This has been a remarkable year.

Good ice—smooth, black, safe—is an uncommon commodity in most years. Building such ice requires cold, of course. But more than that, it requires still days and nights so the wind won't wrinkle the surface. Even given those conditions, good skating ends with the first significant snowfall.

"The big burden of lake skating is that you never

know when it's going to be the last time," Anderson says. "You might only have one day, or one hour."

This winter, the snow held off, allowing skaters a full three weeks of smooth skating.

We're not talking about hockey skaters. Or speed skaters, necessarily. Or skaters etching Olympic-style patterns in a prescribed area.

We are talking about get-out-and-go, see-you-down-the-lake skaters.

For Anderson, the experience is close to rapture. "It's smooth, beautiful, black ice—and then just going on and on."

Sometimes she has trouble finding words for it.

"I just get totally . . ."

"I'm . . ."

"It's . . ."

"It's like I'm passing into a different dimension. The movement is so free. It's like shedding all gravity and being effortless in your movement."

Sometimes, she'll skate long stretches with her eyes closed, just to become immersed in the motion. How far?

"Probably a half-mile on a big lake," she said. "It's like swimming. As long as you've got some equilibrium established, you're OK. And if you do go in circles, big deal."

But mostly, it's worth keeping your eyes open.

"You've got all the visuals," Anderson said. "Light on the ice. Patterns. If there's been some light, dry snow, you have these exquisite and delightful-to-watch patterns of snow blown onto the ice. I'm often reminded of the desert area and sand patterns, the tracks of the wind where it cruises along."

On the Poplar River, up in the bog country where the

water flows gently, Anderson has experienced other visual treats.

"You could skate along on that beautiful, clear, black ice and look down and see the water flowing beneath you and the grasses waving and the trout scurrying along."

One day, she went out to skate and couldn't come home.

"My longest day was six hours. It was a perfect day in terms of physical conditions—20 degrees, so there was no problem staying warm. No wind. Sun for most of the day.

"It was a big lake, and the ice was as good as the ice ever gets. I attempted to come in a couple of times, but I just couldn't let myself."

That's how good it can be, skating the backcountry, in early winter with good ice.

Choppers

Oh, sure. I called myself a Minnesotan.

I had a pair of insulated pac boots. I had heavy-duty jumper cables.

But deep in my heart, I knew I wasn't the real thing.

I didn't own a pair of choppers.

Choppers, in case you were born someplace without fish houses, saunas and lutefisk, are heavy leather mitts worn over wool mittens.

As long as I've lived in Minnesota, nearly all of my friends have worn choppers in the winter. I don't know why it never occurred to me that maybe everyone except me had things figured out. It just didn't.

Then, a couple of months ago, a friend gave me my first pair of choppers. Suddenly, I was a Minnesotan.

I look Minnesotan.

I feel Minnesotan.

I am Minnesotan.

There are, however, some basic differences between me and someone who has been Minnesotan all along. Most choppers you see are crinkled, wrinkled, dark brown, soft and limp. They have taken on a noble look through years of hooking up battery cables, being sat on at the ice rink while skates were laced up, hauling wood from the woodpile to the house, carrying car batteries into the house to warm them up, wrestling snow blowers, pulling snow off the roof, being wrapped around hockey sticks and wiping runny noses.

That's how choppers are supposed to look. Mine are still a creamy yellow, unblemished and a bit stiff.

Choppers have a lot of redeeming qualities. They're tough. They slip on and off easily. They dry out quickly and remain soft.

But those are fringe benefits. The primary virtue of choppers, as the woman in the next cubicle at work put it, is, "They're warm."

Choppers are warm for several reasons, I suppose. One is the inner layer of wool. Hey, sheep may look dumb, but did you ever see one shiver?

The second reason choppers are warm is that they laugh at wind chill factors. They are impervious to moving air.

The third reason, I believe, is on another plane altogether. I think winter respects choppers and the people who wear them. Winter sees a stylish gentleman hustling hunch-shouldered from his car to the hockey arena in some dressy black driving gloves, and winter says to its frigid self: "I'm gonna make that guy regret he has hands."

But winter takes one look at someone wearing chop-pers, someone who shuffles along in no particular hurry, someone appreciating the bracing vigor of a northwest wind, someone with his earflaps pulled down and his long johns pulled up, and winter says, "No sense messing with that guy." And it doesn't.

Another thing about choppers. Watch someone ahead of you walking along wearing a pair. Notice how loosely they fit. This is an essential feature of choppers. Gloves you have to wrestle. The first one goes on easily, but you almost have to take the first one off to get the second one on, and then where are you?

Not choppers. Choppers slide on easily. They shake off quickly. The wonder, then, is how they stay on so well. I think it's a form of loyalty. The way a worn pair of choppers fits reminds me of how an old dog walks beside an old master, looking up occasionally just to make sure he's all right.

Meanwhile, all that extra space between hand and liner and chopper is just more area in which precious body heat circulates, pampering those Minnesotan fin-gers.

One last thing.

My choppers, made by Henry's Shoe Repair in Ely, were crafted from moosehide. I catch myself thinking about that big old lug of a critter hoofing around out there in the woods.

I'm sure he must've felt warm.

For all I know, he might've even felt Minnesotan.

Whiteout

The gray light seeping into the tent told me dawn had come. I shook off sleep and took stock.

Sleeping bag. Warmth. Cold condensation around the tiny opening in the sleeping bag where my nose protruded.

My partner, Dave Olesen, stirred in his bag across the tent. I could hear the rustling of nylon, the wind buffeting our canvas wall tent and the grating of the woodstove's chimney against its base on the stove.

For three days these sounds had greeted us at dawn. We were pinned down by a whiteout storm at the edge of the tundra in Canada's Northwest Territories.

Olesen half-unzipped his sleeping bag, reached out and began stuffing kindling into the woodstove. He scratched a match on the stove's belly and held the flame under the smallest twigs. The fire caught.

We were in no trouble. We had plenty of food. Olesen's 18 sled dogs were well-rested. The temperature held around zero, but we had found enough dead wood among the sparse trees to keep the stove fed and our tent warm.

But the storm, day by day, had whittled away at our travel options. When we left Olesen's cabin on Great Slave Lake we had been bound for a trappers' shack 110 miles away. We had covered 35 miles in two days before the storm forced us to stop. Now we were in the barrenlands, the nearly featureless tundra where trees dare not grow. Olesen had two trapper friends based at the cabin that we had originally set out for. We had reached the fringe of the treeline, where stunted spruces and aging tamaracks yielded to the white expanses, when the whiteout caught us.

For two and a half days now, the wind had been whipping out of the east, off the barrenlands, at 20 to 30 miles per hour day and night. No new snow had fallen, but the tundra winds drove already fallen snow into a ground blizzard that reduced visibility to less than a quarter-mile. Travel eastward into that storm—the direction we needed to go to reach the trappers' shack— was out of the question.

Every few hours throughout the previous couple of days, one or the other of us had left the tent and walked to the top of the nearest ridge. We had wanted to see if the storm was as bad as it seemed. Each time, we returned to our little camp, humbled. It was impossible to keep our eyes open for more than a few seconds in that wind-driven snow.

Even in the shallow depression at the edge of Twin Lakes, where we had sought protection in the last vestiges of the treeline, the wind tormented the tent. Sides and corners of the seven-by-ten-foot wall tent snapped and shuddered in the gusts. Some walls would billow in and others would balloon out. Then a larger gust would invoke a vacuum-like implosion effect to the whole tent.

The snow drifted around the dogs, which were strung out between trees on a stakeout chain. We awoke after our first night in the storm to find Banjo, one of Olesen's Alaskan huskies, sealed to the neck in a drift. Her face was matted with snow. She seemed nonchalant about the matter, but we immediately dug her free.

Over Olesen's high-frequency radio, we talked to his trapper friends on the barrens. The storm was raging where they were, too, 80 miles away. They advised us to be patient, to stay put. They have seen these storms last five days.

Olesen and I passed the time easily. We chopped ice from the frozen lake and heated it over a Coleman stove, making water for ourselves and the dogs. We cut wood. We talked. We sipped tea. We wrote in our journals. We talked some more.

Olesen had seen storms like this on the barrens before. He knew traveling in whiteout conditions, into a wind, was impossible. He had tried it.

"I remember one time two of us were traveling in a whiteout," he told me. "My partner was skiing ahead of the sled, and I was riding the sled. He'd be skiing along, and all of a sudden, he'd fall over.

"I asked him what was wrong, and he said he couldn't keep his balance. I finally said, 'Well, let me ski. You ride the sled.'

"So, I put on the skis. Next thing I knew, I fell over, too."

A whiteout obliterates all reference points.

On that third morning in our universe of light green canvas, Olesen and I ate an oatmeal breakfast, sipped tea into the morning, listened to the tent pop and ripple in the wind, and fed the dogs half a bag of dry dog food.

We had enough dog food for one more day's feeding. Even if the weather cleared, we would have to have two flawless days of 40 miles each to make the trappers' shack. If we made it that far, we would be in good shape. Olesen had flown his Piper Cub out there on skis earlier in the winter and cached some dog food.

On the other hand, if we didn't have two good days of travel—well, we didn't want to think too much about the alternative.

At about mid-morning Olesen suggested we change plans and make a run for his cabin.

"I think once we get back in the trees, the going will be better," he said. "And the way the wind has been blowing for two days, the trail should be blown clear."

The plan was not without risk. Visibility was varying from a hundred to three hundred yards. At times we could see the low ridge on the far side of Twin Lakes. At other times the ridge would disappear entirely behind a veil of snow. If our sleds and dog teams became separated in the blizzard, we would have only one option. Each of us would have to make camp immediately and wait until the storm cleared to find the other.

We always traveled with a tent and food on each sled just in case that possibility became a reality, but neither of us relished the idea of having to use the plan.

Still, Olesen was confident the dogs would lead us to the trail we had come out on and take us home. Behind his reasoning were several years of mushing experience, at least one extended trip on the barrens and two completions of Alaska's 1,150-mile Iditarod Sled Dog Race.

I told Olesen I was willing to give it a try.

There is an almost palpable shift in mood in a camp once a major travel decision has been reached. In this case, a departure time—noon—was set. Immediately, both of us set about doing what needed to be done.

Though there was no hurry or urgency to our movements, there was purpose. We stuffed sleeping bags. We packed food. We dismantled the woodstove. We struck the tent.

Now it was only the two of us, the dogs and the storm. We loaded the two sleds. We harnessed the dogs. We led them yipping and howling to their appointed places along the gangline.

We would leave camp the way we had come in— Olesen and his 10 dogs out front, my sled and eight dogs behind.

Just before we left, Olesen came by my sled and shouted into my ear over the din of the yapping dogs, "When we go out of here, stay pretty close behind me."

He hadn't had to tell me.

He walked to his sled, pulled the knot in the rope that had secured the sled to a sturdy spruce and was off into the whiteness. His sled wasn't 10 yards away from Beaver, my lead dog, when I freed my sled and we bounced over some shoreline drifts in pursuit of Olesen.

Leaving that camp was perhaps the most eerie experience I've ever known in the outdoors. Ahead of us, emerging through the ground blizzard, white land-forms took shape almost like apparitions. I looked back and watched the driven snow swallow our storm camp as if someone were pulling rows of sheer draperies across the landscape.

I looked ahead again. Olesen and his team were just in front. My entire world was eight sled dogs, Olesen's blue anorak and red wind pants—and the white swirling all around us.

The sleds traveled the crusty snow on the lake, then bounced over a marshy area along shore. Suddenly Olesen's leaders put their noses down and veered right. They had found our three-day-old trail. Olesen waited for the rest of his team to make the turn, then looked back at me and raised a mittened fist in the air.

Beaver led my team onto the hard-packed trail and followed Olesen's team west, toward Great Slave Lake.

Silently, and in our separate worlds at that moment, both Olesen and I knew we had it made. The wind had scoured the trail, leaving our sled runner tracks and the dogs' pawprints etched in relief from the trip in. It was going to be a good trip home.

Five hours and 35 miles later, our sleds bounced up the shoreline and into the dog yard at Olesen's homestead on Great Slave.

Brass Tacks

It's the smell that strikes you first. A luscious odor, something between lumber yard and lacquer.

It hits you as soon as you open the door and make the half-step up into the concrete-block building. This is the workplace of Joe Seliga, canoe maker.

Seliga closes the door behind himself and his visitor. He seems glad someone else appreciates the aroma, too. He smiles.

"It's the cedar," he says.

It's a smell Seliga has spent a lot of time with. For 46 of his 72 years, he has built canoes. Wood-canvas canoes, mostly, with cedar ribs and cedar planking. Wood-canvas canoes, like the one taking shape now across the room.

The canoe is upside down, wrapped around the pine

and basswood form that Seliga has been using as a mold for his canoes since 1946. Ribbed and planked now, the canoe-to-be will come off the form today and look at the world right-side up for the first time.

Seliga picks up a tool that looks something like a dandelion digger. He shuffles alongside the inverted craft, using the tool to remove brass tacks that secure the ribs to the form.

Skilled at the act he's performed hundreds of times, he catches each tack as it pops free. When he is finished, he sets the handful of tacks on his workbench. They'll be used again.

It isn't that Seliga is tight; when brass tacks come at $768 per hundred pounds, they aren't wasted.

A canoe maker could use something cheaper than brass tacks, of course. But Seliga would never consider that. That isn't the way he makes canoes.

Across the entire continent, perhaps 60 people still make wood-canvas canoes. That includes the factories, like Old Town in Maine, and the little one-at-a-time folks working in their basements and garages.

Most of the builders haven't met Seliga, but it's safe to say most know of his canoes.

"He builds just a beautiful canoe. Among wood-canvas canoe builders, I don't think anybody is better," says Jeff Dean, president of the Wooden Canoe Heritage Association Ltd., of Madison, Wisconsin. "The quality of his finish is superb, the way the parts meet each other, how carefully it's fit."

That's the kind of reputation that comes with a Seliga canoe.

Over the years, about 45 Seligas have found their way to the canoe livery at Camp Widjiwagan, a wilderness base for the St. Paul YMCA on Burntside Lake north of Ely. The camp has used Old Towns, Chestnuts and a Peterborough, all among the big names in wood-canvas canoes.

David Uher, assistant director of the camp, would take a Seliga every time. "It's flawless. I have yet to see a wood-canvas craft that compares with one of his," Uher says. "He's so far above Old Town, even. You can't see it unless you know what you're looking for."

But it's more than just workmanship. It's a matter of design.

"Joe's inspiration and design was Burt Morris," Dean says. "Joe's the only person I know who's trying to carry that on. In a sense, he's the inheritor of the Morris heritage."

B.N. Morris built canoes in Veazie, Maine, from 1887 through the late 1930s. Seliga grew up with two of them, a 15-footer and an 18-footer his mom and dad owned. When Seliga talks about Morris canoes, he does it with reverence and a faraway look in his eyes.

"I don't think anybody built a finer canoe than B.N. Morris," he says. "It's a canoe that when it gets in the water"—he pauses here for a moment, thinking—"it's like a swan. Proud."

Seliga was the fourth of Steve and Ann Seliga's 12 children. They lived in Ely about a half-mile from Shagawa Lake and, beyond it, the wilderness.

"Dad would pack right from home on White Street to Shagawa and into the woods," Seliga says.

Seliga went along from the beginning.

"Mom would prop me right in the bow," he says.

His earliest memories are of those Morris canoes.

"I remember I'd feel the gunwales and touch the ribs. But I never dreamed I'd build a canoe," he says.

He came into canoe-building accidentally. He still remembers the accident.

He and his dad were in the 18-foot Morris, heading down the Nina Moose River north of Ely on a spring lake trout trip.

"It was in May," Seliga says. "I'm not sure of the year, probably 1934."

The water was high, and Seliga's dad was going to shoot the last set of rapids before Agnes Lake instead of making the portage. Joe took the heaviest pack and started walking the portage.

"All of a sudden, I heard this cracking," Seliga says. "I dropped the pack and went running to the river. I saw Dad. He had hold of an alder and was coming up out of the river. The canoe was upside down in the river.

"The water had been high enough to carry the canoe, all right, but a beaver had dropped an aspen tree across the river. The canoe hit it.

"It broke 21 ribs," Seliga recalls. "We found a jackpine that was kind of hollowed out and put that in along the side. Then we turned around and went home."

Determined to repair the canoe, young Seliga found some cedar and went to work. Using tools and machines at the high school, he formed new ribs and put the canoe back together.

Word of his work spread. A man from Wisconsin had a couple of Old Towns that needed repairing. Seliga protested, but the man insisted. Seliga fixed them up.

"That's when it started, right there," Seliga says.

He decided to build his own canoe, a square-stern to accommodate the outboard motors that were becoming popular then.

"I used to lay in bed and try to figure how I was going

to make a mold, and finally I thought of something," he says.

It took him months to build the mold. Then he built the canoe.

"I had it almost done and a guy from Missouri came by," Joe remembers. "He said, 'I want that canoe.' "

At first Seliga had no intention of selling it.

"I thought, 'This guy's nuts.' Then I thought, 'What the hell, I've got the form made. I can always make myself another one.' "

So, in 1938, he sold the No. 1 Seliga, a 16-foot square-stern, for 40 dollars.

"And I'm still in the hole," he says with a chuckle.

Seliga says a lot of things with a chuckle. He is, one senses, a happy man. The years have been kind to him. A stranger would guess him to be in his late 50s instead of his early 70s.

Uher puts it well.

"He's a fun guy. When you think of him, first off, there's his kind of agelessness. And there's a real sparkle in his eyes and his demeanor."

Seliga isn't big, perhaps 5-foot-10, but his biceps look as if they've spent many an hour swinging a paddle or bending canoe ribs. His hair, cut Army-close, is black on top, graying at the temples. One strand likes to fall across his forehead.

When he's working on a canoe, Seliga most likely will be in a pair of blue jeans, cuffed about two inches at the bottom. Depending on the season, he'll be wearing a colored T-shirt or colored sweatshirt, both on the loose side.

Seliga doesn't like to talk about how many canoes he's made over the years. Nor does he like to talk about price. He remembers selling canoes for $135, then $150 and later $175.

He never did it for a living. Never could have, he says.

"No way I could make it go. I couldn't even meet expenses. I'd have died on the vine," he says. "It's been a hobby. I did it at my convenience and pleasure only."

That's the way he's doing it now. He isn't looking for business. The canoes he's making today, he says, are for his nine grandchildren.

Through the years, he made enough money to support his hobby by working at the Zenith iron mine in Ely and Reserve's taconite operation in Babbitt.

His son, Richard, helped him with the canoe building until he graduated from high school.

"That's when my trusty helper came in," Seliga says.

He's talking about Nora, His wife of 52 years.

"She's my right hand," he says. "She always finds time to come in here and give me a hand."

Nora is reticent about her role in the partnership. Those who know the Seligas aren't so hesitant to discuss it.

"Nora's as involved as he is," says Widjiwagan's Uher. "She's that second set of hands when they're needed so much."

Like when it's time to tack the planking to a set of ribs. A 17-foot canoe is built around some 50 ribs. It takes a lot of tacks to apply the 3-inch strips of planking to those ribs.

"About three thousand," she says. "I sort of counted 'em one day."

Persistence in the face of such tedium is the hallmark of the wood-canvas canoe-building process.

The building of a canoe, however, is often simpler than finding the materials for it. Seliga has trouble finding wood that measures up to his standards. He searches lumber yards east to Hovland; north to Fort Frances, Ontario; west to Kelliher, Minnesota; and south to Duluth in search of good white cedar.

"Last summer I made three trips," Seliga says. "One day I came back with 25 dollars worth. Another day I came back with 30 dollars worth. The third day, nothing. I spend more money looking for the stuff than I do on the materials."

White cedar is for ribs and planking. Then there's black ash for the stem pieces and the cane seats, sitka spruce for the gunwales, cherry for the decks.

His current batch of spruce came from Alaska, with a friend of a friend. Last summer, he drove to Winnipeg to find some.

He makes virtually every part of his canoes from the cane seats to the yoke pads. It is a labor he loves.

"It's the wood, and the results you can get out of it," he says. "The beauty of it.

"I always felt if I couldn't do that, if I couldn't make it come out the way I wanted, as far as I was concerned there was no use even doing it."

Now, on this afternoon, he is ready to take his ribbed-and-planked canoe off its form. He solicits the help of his visitor, saving Nora a trip to the shop.

The bow is popped off first, then the stern. Then the fragile shell is rolled over and set upright on the form.

To handle the rudimentary craft is to hold a living creature of sorts. Here is a sense of life, of personality.

Seliga knows the feeling. So do those who've paddled his canoes.

"Sandy Bridges, when he used to guide for the Boy Scouts of America, he'd say, 'You know, Joe, I just go down that lake talking to that canoe,' " Seliga says.

He squints and holds his hands in front of him, embracing the thought.

"That's the thing, there," he says. "You can talk to that thing. I'm not knockin' aluminum, but you haven't got anything there that's alive."

Behind him, hanging on a rack over his workbench, hangs another canoe in the works. This one is further along, already wrapped in canvas.

Seliga and his visitor take it down and set it gently on two carpet-covered sawhorses.

The canoe's interior ribs and planking gleam under three coats of varnish. Standing next to the canoe, Seliga is off on another story now. As he speaks, he strokes the inside of the canoe. He isn't aware that he's doing this. It's done subconsciously, like a kid throwing a baseball idly into his mitt, just because it feels good.

It must be something like the way he rubbed the ribs and planks of those Morris canoes of his childhood.

He is asked again about those canoes, and about what he said of them, that no one ever built a nicer canoe. He's asked how he thinks a Seliga would stack up.

"I'm not saying," he says.

Then he gets that squinty, faraway look in his eyes again.

Dreaming

A walleye shore lunch. That's what I'm thinking about.

It is deep winter and gray and cold, and I want a chunk of yellow-gold walleye sizzling in a cast-iron skillet, and I want it now.

Is it just me, or did Cabin Fever set in for real all over the North sometime in the past three days?

I can see this shore lunch so clearly. I am sitting on a loaf of granite. My boat is nosed up into the weeds at the water's edge, tied to a birch tree, and the leaves are rustling in the breeze.

Someone is touching a match to the fire, built in a nest of rocks on the granite. The frying pan will go on soon, followed by the potatoes and, finally, the fish.

The fish.

Someone is turning them into fillets now, working with precise strokes of the knife, peeling that luscious pink meat away from the rib cage, not wasting an ounce. We'll rinse the fillets in the lake and deliver them in a plastic bag to the cook. He'll be kneeling at the fire tossing on an occasional stick of wood.

A white-throated sparrow will call from a nearby island, and a wool shirt will feel good even at midday.

Oh, and the water. I can see that, too. It'll be deep blue and clean and cold. The breeze will be ruffling it some, just enough to rock the boat at its mooring and make the waves talk when they meet the granite.

I'm not sure what triggered all of this in me. Maybe it was the collection of maps an old man gave me this week. I spent some time poring over those when I should have been doing something productive.

Or maybe it was the fishing magazine that arrived in my morning mail, making promises only fishing magazines make.

Bass-Breakthrough Lure Revealed.

Crappies—Guaranteed Patterns.

Pike—Surefire System.

When I read those headlines in deep winter, I believe.

Or possibly my mind was set to wandering by the changing angle of the sun as it picks its way through the buildings of downtown Duluth. Already it is noticeably higher than it was a few weeks ago. What this change sets off in the synapses of my brain cells, I don't know.

It is the same urge that makes us march like lemmings to boat shows and fishing clinics. It makes us lie down beside the still waters of Saturday's outdoor TV shows and watch Al and Babe and Roland and Jerry run last summer's vacation movies. It makes us sit down with buddies at lunch and begin making lists.

Tent. Rain fly. Ax. Saw. Grate. Griddle.

Hash browns. Bacon. Oatmeal. Venison steaks. Fish breading.

Ah, fish breading.

I think the fire is about right now. The potatoes are nicely browned. The cook sets them to the side to keep warm. He shakes a walleye fillet in the breading—corn meal, flour, lemon pepper. He lays the fish in the hot grease and the skillet starts to sing. Another fillet, more sizzle, until the whole skillet is sputtering with life.

The first gull arrives for the fish carcasses on the rock. It lands just offshore, as gulls always do, and paddles in to inspect the offerings.

The cook flips the fillets now, and it's time to find plates. There they are, in the old canvas cook-set bag.

Now. It's time. The cook serves up the fillets. He heaps on the spuds. We grab cups and scoop up lake water. We find chairs in the granite.

Yes. That first bite. Hot and crisp and—walleye!

Might as well just moan. You don't need to say anything. Everyone else knows just what you're thinking.

Lake. Sky. Walleye. Rock.

Shore lunch.

I know it's February.

But we can dream.

Spring

The Un-Season
South and North
Catch of the Day
Pushing It
Simply Sauna

The Un-Season

It's that season again.

Not Winter and Not Summer.

Oh, I know. People in other places have an actual name for this time of year. But here in the North, we don't use that name much.

Up here, this time of year isn't so much a season as the absence of one—a long, vague period that starts somewhere in March and lasts into June.

In other parts of the country, this season is defined by the poking up of tulips, or the unfurling of jonquils or the lazy bobbing of lilac blossoms on a warm breeze.

Well, we would love to call that time of year spring here in the North Country. But if we did, we'd be cheating ourselves out of what we like to call summer. So, we apply the concept of spring to everything from late ice-fishing trips to pre-mosquito camping trips in June.

Granted, it's a loose concept. But like the long johns we've worn all winter, the concept is one we've grown comfortable with, and we aren't likely to shed it soon. I guess the same goes for the long johns.

Up here, spring can mean skiing in for lake trout through the ice on the lakes up in Canada, where lake trout can legally be taken any time after January first. You can tell it's a spring trip because daylight lasts almost 12 hours, and you can figure on traveling atop a firm layer of crusted snow.

That's spring.

Somebody else might choose to spend the same day fishing open water on the Lower Brule River in Wisconsin, hoping to fool a steelhead with a piece of orange yarn. There will be ice fast to the shoreline, and the river temperature might have to struggle to get out of the 30s.

But it's spring. The steelheaders are back on the Brule.

Spring can be especially cruel on the shores of Lake Superior. It might be 65 and sunny up on the hill, but if the wind's out of the east, it'll be 45 with a wind chill of about 31 down at Brighton Beach. But you can bet, if it's a Saturday in April, some family will be down there trying to have a picnic. It isn't easy, what with Mom and Dad and the four kids all in the family sedan passing pieces of chicken back and forth.

But, hey, it's spring in Duluth.

While people in other parts of the country can't wait for Memorial Day so the city swimming pools will be filled with water, we spend that weekend staring at rows of felt-lined pac boots in the entry hall having quiet debates with ourselves.

"Might as well put those away for the summer."

"Well, then again, better not."

"Ah, heck. It's almost June."

"Right. It's almost June."

And so, you leave them out. And once or twice more that season, you're glad you did.

People in the Deep South—Iowa, Indiana, South Dakota—spend spring planting peas and snipping tulips. Up here, we sit on pins and needles waiting for pebbles on the shore of Lake Superior to begin reappearing through Swiss cheese slabs of ice. We walk in the woods and are overjoyed to see snow fleas—the tiny black specks that emerge to seek warmth at 40 degrees. We spend cozy nights in front of the woodstove sorting our fishing tackle—a week before the season opens.

Not Winter and Not Summer isn't bad if all your relatives live up here. What's almost intolerable is having relatives near the Equator—in, say, Kansas, Missouri or Kentucky. They know what we're suffering through up here in April because the letters we send them are sometimes smudged with paw prints from the sled dogs we used to get outgoing mail to the post office.

These otherwise kind relatives delight in calling at the end of March to tell us they've picked their first peas. Really. Of course, we can't talk long. We're too preoccupied wondering if the "budget" payments we've made to the fuel oil company all winter were ample enough that we'll come out even by July.

What's crazy is that we stay. We know it's going to be this way each year in Not Winter and Not Summer. And we stay.

I'm not sure why you stay. But I know why I do. Each year, 'long about the end of Not Winter and Not Summer, I inhale my first blackfly.

And I know the wait has been worthwhile.

South and North

The canoe slid around the crook in the river and the mallards saw us. The drake lifted off first, beating the air with those big wings, pulling up his orange landing gear as he rose. The hen came off just behind him, delivering us a verbal spanking as she left.

Then, from farther ahead, came a pair of wood ducks from the other side of the river. Unlike the mallards, they took off low and stayed that way. They made a sound that was part squeal, part whimper. Somewhere up ahead, they tucked into the brush, and we knew we would see them again.

We might have talked to each other, Phyllis and I. We might have remarked at the wariness of the mallards or the call of the woodies. We might have, but we had long since quit talking about the riverside spectacles. We were simply content to appreciate, over and over again, the explosion of waterfowl at every bend.

We had stolen two days in April on the Namekagon and St. Croix rivers of northwestern Wisconsin. We had come seeking the feel of moving water and a snug camp on the riverbank. We found ourselves moving south through a world of waterfowl moving north.

The old river canoe, a weathered Old Town, nosed around another bend. Mallards from the left. Woodies on the right. A fleet of goldeneyes whistling overhead.

This wasn't the mature spring of late April. This was the first weekend of the month. We shouldn't have been enjoying 85-degree highs and worrying about sunburns. Having set the weekend aside for a getaway, we thought about going north from our home in Duluth and snowshoeing in to a remote cabin not far from the Canadian border.

But at midweek, when we had heard projections for unseasonable warmth, we began looking south. Now we were sliding through Burnett County, Wisconsin, on this artery of icewater, one of the jewels of the country's National Wild and Scenic Rivers network.

Locals told us the river was high—full of leftover winter. We would be paddling 35 miles of river, most of them on the Namekagon and the final few on the wide St. Croix.

Looking at the woods, you might have thought it was November. None of the hardwoods had begun to consider making leaves. Not a sprig of green sprang anywhere from the forest floor. The forest looked much as it must have in deer season, with a single exception— the angle of the sun.

The November sun comes slanting low and thin. This sun came splashing down from high in the Norway pines. It sparkled on the riffles of the river. It reflected colors from the dark end of the spectrum on the wings of every flushing mallard. And come late afternoon, it was in no hurry to drop over the edge of the world on its way to morning.

Nor was the Namekagon in any rush to deliver its payload to the St. Croix, which would eventually send it on down to the Mississippi and the Gulf of Mexico. The little river snaked north and west and sometimes back east on its way south. It is a river meant for canoes, quick and smooth and wild in the Wisconsin sense of the word. That is to say, with a road crossing here and a deer shack there, you weren't going to mistake the waterway for something in the Northwest Territories.

But then again, it was April, and we were paddling, and there was, at that moment, a bald eagle drawing lazy circles against the sky overhead.

This eagle was not the first we had seen, and it wouldn't be the last. Eagles, too, were moving north as we moved south. They were following the open water that meant fresh fish, or maybe fresh duck.

In our two days in April on these rivers, we would see eagles, hundreds of ducks, an osprey, a great blue heron, two beavers, a woodchuck, a muskrat, a pair of porcupines and several white-tailed deer.

We camped that night on an outside bend of the river at the foot of a handsome ridge. We cooked dinner over a fire of white pine that winter's snows had pruned from the forest. We kept the teapot on and the fire dancing long after dusk. We sat close together, leaned on a piece of deadfall and wondered at the good fortune that allowed us to be paddling before wood tick season.

We decided, sitting there watching the flames lick the black night, that we would get up early in the morning and paddle a few miles before breakfast. It just seemed like the right thing to do.

When daylight came, I lay in my sleeping bag for a while waiting for Phyllis to stir. I heard a beaver slap its tail on the water, a Canada goose honking just upstream and a ruffed grouse trying to drum up a mate somewhere in the woods.

It was going to be another good day, moving south while spring moved north.

Catch of the Day

This one felt good.

My jig and minnow had been right on the bottom when it hit, and it hadn't given any ground yet.

Other than one initial lateral run, it had stayed right beneath the boat and fought like a bulldog.

Once a year, or every two years, you get into a battle like this one.

In the stern of his 14-foot boat, Vernon "Hunch" Carlson shared my anticipation as he watched my fishing rod throb.

We were in 15 feet of water, just off a small island near Birch Point on Lake Vermilion. We had found a few small walleyes, but this one had to be somebody's mama. This baby liked living 15 feet below the surface and wasn't high on the idea of seeing any daylight.

Small waves pushed by a southeasterly wind bounced the boat, contributing to the action.

I don't get a chance to play big fish often, and I was doing my best to be cool about it. I knew that four anglers in a nearby boat were watching, and I was trying—unsuccessfully—not to think about my audience. Already I had loosened my drag, so that a sudden run wouldn't snap my four-pound-test line. I was back-reeling the way I'd seen Al and Babe and the big boys do it on TV.

Most of all, this was fun. You get that feeling up in your throat, and you sort of giggle to yourself, and you can't help but think that this is what makes people love fishing.

I was thinking about all of that and trying not to watch the people watching me when I caught my first sight of something at the end of my line.

Funny, I thought, the eyes don't look right on that fish. And they're lined up in a weird sort of way. They were round, all right, and green. But they didn't come in a left and a right. They came in a row, spaced apart, almost like the guides on a . . .

Fishing rod.

Uh-huh. I had been fighting an algae-coated fishing rod and a slime-covered Zebco reel.

I'd guess the vintage at the early '80s. The rod was broken above the third guide. My jig was hooked into one of the guides. The rod wasn't going to get away.

Which meant, of course, that I was going to have to land it. Which I did, much to the amusement of Hunch Carlson.

I never did make eye contact with the people in the other boat.

Pushing It

The trip is beginning to take shape. Two of us will go, maybe four. No more.

We'll have five days.

We'll get up in the middle of the night and drive north. It will be later than we planned when we get to the lake. It always is. But no matter what time it is, we'll put the canoes in and start paddling into Ontario's Quetico Provincial Park.

My hunch is that we'll paddle until the mosquitoes come out that night, and likely as not we'll make camp in the dark. We'll be that fired up.

We need this trip.

We've made some short trips. We've gone back to the easy places. We've done the family trips where being there is much more important than getting somewhere else.

As good as those trips have been, as essential as they are, it is time for something else. It is time to cover some ground, to make some miles, to see some new country.

We didn't come at this trip with that in mind, but when we sat down to talk about what we wanted to do, we found that we had the same thing in mind.

"I was thinking we might drive up to the north side of the Quetico," one friend said, "and paddle back down."

Funny. That's exactly what I'd been thinking.

The proposal was not without some hitches. It would mean a long drive to the put-in. It would mean arranging a pickup on the other end. It would mean a lot of miles to paddle in five days.

I could see the intensity in my friend's eyes as he embraced the idea. As I was, he was ready to push himself.

It is one thing to do a trip for the sake of merely making miles. That is not what we are up to. Nor will we unwittingly plan a trip that, once embarked upon, turns out to be more than we wanted. We have all made those mistakes in the past.

Some times, though, it feels right to bite off a little more than you're accustomed to chewing.

We know we'll be putting in long days on this trip. We know we won't be doing as much fishing as we'd normally do. We can expect, somewhere along the way, to get in some minor jam that will make for an early-morning-start or a late-evening paddle, or maybe both in the same day.

Let us have it. We're ready.

I, for one, will be ready to stumble straight from the dinner fire to the sleeping bag on a night or two. I'll be ready to navigate in unfamiliar country, spending the day matching squiggly lines on the map with the shoreline and islands we're passing.

I'll be ready to live with wet feet and cracked hands and a smoke-smudged face for five days straight. I'll be ready to buck some waves and make fire in the rain and let some mosquitoes find the sweet spot in my back on a portage.

I don't know for sure where this urge comes from. It is not a macho thing. It will not be done for the sake of talking about it later. I only know that for me, for now, it feels right.

My buddies are saying the same thing.

One of these nights now, we'll lay out the maps. We'll trace the options with a sharp pencil. We'll debate the merits of one route over another.

Those are merely refinements. The basics are set. We'll paddle down through Quetico. We'll have our work cut out for us.

We'll love it.

Simply Sauna

I stood alone on the dock and listened to the sound of lake water dripping from my naked body onto the cedar planks.

It was a good sound—soft and irregular and natural.

I looked up and drank in the night sky, pitch black overhead, still blue-black along the western horizon at 10:30. Behind me, along the lakeshore, butterscotch light flowed out of the sauna window.

The old log sauna had been sitting on that lakeshore longer than I'd been alive. It had, no doubt, seen a few docks come and go. I wondered how many times it had heard the evening exhortations of its users—the thumping of feet down the dock, the splash in the lake, the hoots of healthy stimulation.

It all seemed so right—the squat little sauna, the cabin up the hill, the lake, the stars, the water dripping onto the dock.

We had come north for a week on the lake. A week at the cabin. A week in which water and sky and red pines became the overriding presence in our lives. A week without deadlines or commitments or cares.

The cabin was not ours, but friends had graciously let us adopt it for a few days. We had been there many times before, enough times to know the gentle pitch of its floors, the moss growing on the steps that led down from the driveway and the aroma of the woodshed.

I have not considered myself a cabin person. I always figured I'd rather spend my weeks off paddling the labyrinth of waters that lead north from this lake to where the roads quit. But with a five-month-old who was more intent on growing teeth than hair, we had decided not to spend the week living in a nylon shelter measuring six feet by eight.

Oh, was that a good decision.

Now the five-month-old was snoozing, fenced in by rolled-up blankets on the double bed, and his six-year-old sister was tucked in just a room away. For their mother and me, the night had become the purest form of what we had come north seeking—simplicity.

Dock. Lake. Sky. Silence.

The cabin will do that for you, if you let it. You slip into it that first day like putting on an old flannel shirt, and it feels so good.

Part of the feeling is the cabin itself. The furniture is mostly hand-me-downs from parents and grandparents. The dishes don't match. The pull string for the bathroom light is still an old fishing sinker suspended on dacron fishing line. Fly rods, nothing fancy, hang on the ceiling beams. A hummingbird feeder hangs outside the window.

You ease into cabin time. This is the delicious state in which your wristwatch blinks idly from the kitchen table all week. You don't care whether you eat lunch or walk down to the dock to see if the mallards are around or collect blown-down birch branches for the evening bonfire.

If you get highly motivated, you might perform some essential chore such as refilling the hummingbird feeder.

On cabin time, you can do all of the things you want to do back home but usually don't. Like grabbing the six-year-old on her way across the room, sweeping her off her feet and smothering her with kisses. Just because. Or hugging your wife for no apparent reason. Or letting a nap wash over you as you lie on the couch with no regard for what time you might reawaken.

You think about all of that as you stand on the dock, contemplating the universe. You think that this is how the first people lived, with an ear for night sounds and a feel for the land and a knowledge of the sky. You wish—or you think you do—that it could be that way again. Simple and timeless and with a closeness to the Earth.

You think about that and you realize, eventually, that the water has stopped dripping now, and that you are cooling in the night air, and that it is time for more heat.

Summer

Batchewaung

We had seen the rain coming while we were sitting on rocks, eating granola around the breakfast fire in Pickerel Narrows. The sky had looked bruised in the west and south, and the air had had a weight to it.

Now the four of us were stroking across Batchewaung Lake, and the rain had found us.

It was a needle-fine rain, the kind of rain you confuse with mist in the city. But out here, on the waters of Ontario's Quetico Provincial Park, there was no mistaking it. The glassy surface of Batchewaung was dappled with millions of tiny dimples, each the final resting place of a microdrop from the heavens.

It was not the kind of rain that was going to send any of us digging into a Duluth pack for rain gear. The air was warm and thick. And we were headed for Nym Lake, our take-out point, after five days on the trail.

No use worrying about staying dry now. Let it rain. Let those fine drops form tiny rivers on our tanned skin. Let those rivers flow down our backs and arms. Let the accumulated beads of liquid cling to the bills of our caps and soak the legs of our pants.

Though none of us said it, there was an unmistakable sense that we could handle anything at this point. We were at home on the water, at peace with the country we had been traveling through, trail-toughened, confident.

We edged away from the protection of a narrow bay and into the open reaches of Batchewaung.

Batchewaung is a big lake by Quetico standards, and it can send you paddling for cover in a good blow. The wind was building from the southeast, quartering us, and we were keeping an eye on it.

Our most direct line would take us slanting past some gull nesting rocks in the middle of the lake, then to a sand beach that marked the portage into Nym.

Ahead and off to one side, Dave and Tom looked good moving across the lake, paddles swinging in quick tempo, strokes synchronized bow and stern.

Dan and I glided along, lost in the concentration of our paddling, switching sides on Dan's cues from the stern, listening to the waves slap at the bow. We spoke occasionally, but mostly we swung paddles, licked rain and reveled in the feeling that comes only after several days in the bush.

We had left the dock on Nym five days ago, but now it seemed like a couple of weeks. We had fought winds on Oriana Lake, paddled up on a bull moose in velvet on South Twin Lake and watched a windstorm prune dead trees on an island in Bent Pine. We had eaten fresh walleyes and bass every night, surprised a juvenile black bear tearing apart an old stump and dipped our drinking water from over the side of the canoe.

At midday rests, we had swum naked. At night we had steeped tea over hot fires on ancient campsites. We had come to know the old feelings—Duluth pack straps digging into shoulders, bog ooze sucking at boots, woodsmoke stinging the eyes. We had become familiar with the old sounds—rain drilling a tent fly, waterfalls at a distance, wingbeats of ravens.

We had, in short, immersed ourselves in the country we love.

Once we had fallen into the rhythm of the land, everything had become so simple. The paddlers in the lead canoe would scout a campsite. We'd unload, pitch tents, snack on caramels and gather firewood. Dave and Tom would tend the fire and bring a mountain of potatoes and onions to a sizzling brown. Dan and I would paddle down the shore, locate some cooperative walleyes or bass, fillet them out and paddle back.

Dave and Tom would have the water boiling when we returned to camp, and the cubes of fresh fish would be dropped in. Five minutes later, we would find some soft rocks and watch the sun slide down the sky as we put away the best food any of us had ever tasted.

There comes a time on such a trip, along about the fourth day, when you feel as if you could do this forever. It would be the four of us, just cruising Quetico for a month, two months, whatever. Escorted by eagles, resupplied by outposts on the fringe, we would simply travel—and travel simply—until we knew every pocket of that wonderful country. Up in Trousers and Cache and McKenzie. Down in Bit, Bell, Fran and Slate. Over on La Croix and Tanner and Poohbah. Up on Beaver-house, Cirrus and McAlpine.

No portage would be too tough, for there would be time, plenty of time. No perfect island campsite would have to be paddled by, for there would always be another night and another camp. No Indian rock paint-ings would be too far off the beaten path to inspect.

Ah, but in reality there were spouses and little people and jobs waiting, and there we were, paddling across Batchewaung toward the end of our trip.

The rain came harder. Everything was wet. Warm rain poured down the backs of our necks and trickled down the valleys of our backbones.

We edged the canoes toward the sand beach, stepped into shallows over our boot tops and began the final carry to Nym.

Rock of Ages

It was early in the morning and the cool was still coming out of the shadowy places. I walked past quiet homes with newspapers freshly deposited on their front porches.

I was looking for an outcropping of rock near the edge of Hartley Park.

The rock isn't far from my home. I had first seen the rock a few months ago while I was driving to work. Now I try to catch a glimpse of it in the mornings on my way down the hill to work.

I had always thought the rock would be a good place to sit, to survey my neighborhood and to think.

Although I know Hartley Park from running and hiking and skiing its trails, I had never found this specific outcrop in my scurryings. Today, I figured, I'd go looking for it.

I left the street and dipped into the park, trying to take a line that would deliver me to the rock face. Along the way, I passed familiar landmarks—Tischer Creek, the wood-chipped ski trail, a rocky running trail. At the top of a steep climb, I figured I must be close. I struck off in a new direction toward where the rock had to be.

A grassy trail fringed with hawkweed and butterflies guided me on. Then the forest canopy opened, and I was there.

I sat down on a few tons of basalt and looked around.

The rock face rose about 50 feet from the forest floor. That put me, on top, a good 20 feet above the crowns of birch and basswood trees. The cliff provided nearly a 180-degree sweep of the park and the Woodland neighborhood. Homes poked through the trees in spots. In the distance I could see part of a pond and windrows of tombstones at a cemetery.

Woodland Avenue, a main artery in this part of town, serpentined down the hill, then disappeared in the forest. All in all, except for two water towers on the horizon, the panorama was a pleasant one.

I sat down. Already this July morning was warm. A light breeze, the kind hawks look for, rose along the edge of the rock face. I peeled off my sweater.

It felt good to be there after wondering about the place for so long and seeing it from a distance so often. It wasn't hard to find, and I'm sure many other people had stood on this same piece of Earth. The little trail leading to the spot told me that much. Still, it was enough of a walk that you could probably figure on being alone when you came here. I liked that.

A gull flew down the valley over Tischer Creek and

veered off toward the cemetery. Somewhere in the distance a small dog barked.

I'm not sure what it is that makes sitting in high places so pleasant. It just is. Part of the satisfaction must be that it's so unusual to let your gaze drift over a mile or two of countryside. We spend too much time these days staring close-range at screens that blink green numbers at us.

Part of the pleasure, too, is that it's enjoyable to look down on the things you normally look up at—trees, for instance. Being up high, you get a good feeling for how much fun it would be to be a bird on a day like this.

As cliffs go, this one is modest. It is probably not high enough to lure a peregrine falcon to nest. It doesn't give you the blue of Lake Superior that the Greenstone Ridge on Isle Royale does.

But locations like those aren't just a 20-minute walk from home, either. It is one thing to drive through the night and walk part of the morning to a place you know is going to take your breath away. It is something else to know, on any given day, that a good sitting rock is close by.

As I sat there, I couldn't help thinking about my grandfather. He died about 20 years ago, but I used to spend summer nights at the farm where he and my grandmother lived. I remember waking up early on those hot mornings, walking into his bedroom and seeing him sitting there on a hard-backed chair, looking out his second-story window.

He would be smoking a Chesterfield, and the ashtray would be on the windowsill. The window was shoved all the way up, and he was staring through the screen, looking at his cattle and Shetland ponies in the pasture.

No telling how long he'd been there. He was always up before anybody else.

Being a kid, I never could figure why anyone would just want to sit at a window and stare out, but now, here on the rock, I began to understand. It felt good, being up high, looking at nothing, letting my thoughts drift. And although any time of day is good to do that, mornings are best. You spend half an hour up high, early in the day, thinking about nothing, and you've gotten your day off to a good start.

I don't know how much being up high had to do with my grandpa's window sitting, but I never saw him do it on the first floor.

I thought a lot about my grandfather while I was on the rock. About the old L.C. Smith shotguns he kept in the corner of his room. About riding through hayfields in a pickup with him. About the straw hats he wore. I hadn't thought about those things for a long time.

I could see I was going to spend more time on that rock in the days ahead. I had other things that needed thinking about.

But that was enough for one day. I picked up my sweater and headed off past the hawkweed for home.

Army Worms

Lots of people think we enjoy four invigorating seasons here in the North Country.

That is wrong.

We have five seasons, and I can name them for you: Winter, Ticks, Blackflies, Mosquitoes and Army Worms.

The greatest of these is Army Worms.

Oh, winter is significant. But you can deal with winter. It lasts eight or nine months. We've developed a lifestyle around winter. You can buy stuff that throws it and shoves it and lifts it and melts it.

Army worms are too temporary to deal with. No self-respecting entrepreneur is going to develop a machine to throw army worms into your neighbor's yard. Businesses could sell wormthrowers for only three weeks a year. Then they'd have to spin a cocoon and wait out the off-season.

So we're stuck with these critters that are too short to mow, too soft to sweep and too sticky to flick.

Let's get something straight here. I'm a nature kind of guy. I like most things that slither and creep and swim and hoot. I don't put salt on slugs. I don't turn the hose on cats. I touch leeches.

But I'll tell you something about these army worms. I hate 'em. I don't hate them individually. But collectively, they are driving me wacko.

I reach down to tie my shoe. Squish. Army worm on the shoestring.

I reach under the canoe to flip it over. Squish. Army worm on the gunwale.

I reach out to get the mail. Squish. Army worm on the mailbox lid.

Walk outside. You think it's raining. But wait a minute—the sun's out. Those aren't raindrops. Those are billions and billions of tiny, hard specks falling out of the trees. Not army worms, but army worm extract— the stuff that comes out the back end of army worms when they're through digesting your aspen tree.

Try to barbecue a coho salmon on your Weber under that kind of fallout. No, honey. That's not lemon pepper on your fillet. That's *salmon a la wormeaux l'aimee*, my love. And it's high in fiber.

I went for a bike ride during the peak of the worm movement. The road stank. No lie. It smelled sort of like hot raisins and burned flesh. I must have run over thousands of them with my skinny tires. You know what? They pop. How can something so squishy and mooshy and spineless pop?

But those were the good old days, when the army worms were just denuding the countryside. Now they have become very, very sleepy. And so, they are busy making themselves little tiny sleeping bags. Isn't that precious? We found one between a cabinet and the carpet in our family room. In our house! No problem. I shot it with my 12-gauge. No fuss. No muss. (Just kidding.)

These cocoons are everywhere. I swear if you'd happen to fall asleep out in the yard, you'd wake up with army worm cocoons in your armpits.

Try to sweep the cocoons from your eaves or your siding or your armpits and you'll learn another fascinating fact about army worms. As soon as they start spinning these indestructible webs, their bodies become basically a quivering blob of brown liquid.

Sure, you can sweep them off your house. And your house suddenly looks as if the entire roster of major league baseball players has been invited over to practice tobacco spitting.

Your other choice is not to sweep but to wait and remove the little yellow sleeping bags later. That's when you'll learn that DuPont has yet to create a fabric with the tenacity, integrity and tensile strength of an army worm cocoon. I recommend a chisel.

But at least the cocooning of my home signals the end of the gooshy season.

That means just one thing—time to change the oil in the snowblower.

Winter's coming on.

High Summer

My friend calls it high summer. I think I know what he means.

At the apogee of summer—remember being at the top of a double Ferris wheel?—summer seems to stand still and exist forever.

It is not coming-on summer, when all is lush and succulent and bursting with new life. It is beyond that. It is the time of year that seems to say, "OK. This is it. It isn't going to get any greener than this. Soak it up. Enjoy it."

Which is what my friend was doing one night a couple of weeks ago. His wife and kids were in bed. He had stayed up to do some work around the house. At one o'clock he decided to sit out in the front yard for a few moments before going to bed.

He had picked one of those idyllic summer evenings. Warm enough that a breeze felt good. Bugless, at least the way we define that blissful condition here in the North.

My friend sat out for some time, watching the stars and the blackness over Lake Superior. He said five ships passed in the night while he sat there. That should tell you he was out for quite a while.

"When I went up the stairs to go to bed, I noticed it was getting light in the east," he said.

High summer. That's what it'll do to you. You sit down on your front porch or a rock at a campsite or a cliff over Lake Superior, and you stay there. You stay there because being there is too good to do anything else.

All you want to do is let that soft air drift over your arms and watch another star fall and never forget the feeling you're feeling.

I can remember coming home many nights last winter listening to the voice of a three-year-old asking, "When is it going to be summer again?" I would say, "It will be a long time." And it was.

Yet now that it's here, and has been for so long, it seems as if winter had been merely something we read about in a book. Could it have been that cold? Could it have grown dark so early each afternoon? Could it have lasted so long? In high summer, you begin to wonder.

As seasons go, high summer is subtle. It's as much a feeling as a definable few weeks on the calendar. Yet its evidence is tangible.

High summer is Winnebagos on the road and wasps in the eaves and Iowans in your town. It's bugs on the windshield and a canoe on the roof and potato salad in the cooler in the trunk. It's fireweed and tansy and restaurants that serve iced tea again.

High summer is fresh raspberries on your cereal and the Little League all-star game and a mama grouse with three half-grown young.

It's precious. Because even when it seems high summer could last forever, when you finally feel as if you've gone fishing as much as you said you would, when you've put off the painting three times and still managed to get it done—you begin to feel an undercurrent of anxiety.

Because you know, deep in your Northern heart, that high summer can't last forever. One day, any time now, you'll see the first hint of red on a swatch of maple leaves. You'll see the first aspen leaves splashed on a forest trail. You'll smell something that reminds you more of grouse hunting than bicycling.

One night, getting ready to walk the dog, you'll reach for your wool shirt. And high summer will be gone.

But we'll have time to talk about that later. For now, let it be enough to sit on a log, ponder profound questions and study a bug beside your boot.

High summer is upon us. Savor it.

Little Hand, Big Hand

We hadn't done much of anything, really.

We had climbed some rocks. We had eaten Rice-a-Roni. We had built a campfire.

When one of you is fortysomething and the other is six, you don't need to do much on a camping trip. You just need to hang out, together, and see what happens.

I'm not sure what happens when one parent and one child go off by themselves for a couple of days, but I can tell you it is good. Child psychiatrists probably have a term for it. Maybe adult psychiatrists have a term for it, too. I don't want to know about the jargon or the theory.

All I know is that the six-year-old and I had done more hand-in-hand walking in the previous 24 hours than we had for about the past six months. We'd walk along, to the outhouse or the tadpole pond or the pebble beach, and we'd talk about whatever came to mind.

Which, when you're six, can be almost anything.

Sometimes, we'd walk and not talk, which was just as good.

A six-year-old's hand fits nicely into a dad's hand. The little hand is sort of soft, and sometimes a little tacky with sweat, but it feels good riding there and I'm guessing it might not be too many more years before that little girl wouldn't be caught dead holding her dad's hand.

So I made the most of those simple moments. We read her book by the light of a headlamp in the tent, and after she went to sleep I went to the edge of camp and watched an ore boat twinkling its way down the lake.

The next day we packed up the stove, folded the tent and headed for the highway. We were thinking about one more night of camping somewhere along the shore of Lake Superior. I should have sensed the pangs for home when we were putting away the tent.

"I sure like our tent, don't you?" I said, just making conversation.

"Yeah," she said, "but I miss Mom in a way."

We went to the rock shop and we stopped at a restaurant for a cinnamon roll and we talked about the rest of our day. The six-year-old thought she might be ready to call it a trip and go home.

I said that would be fine. No point in force-marching a kid up the shore, I figured.

We were maybe 10 miles down the road toward home when there came a small voice from the back seat.

"Dad, I think I want to go camping some more," the voice said. Hey, Dad was flexible. I told her we could still go camping. She said that's what she wanted to do. She was sure.

So, I turned the truck around and headed up the shore again. We were going camping. We'd find a campground and have another 24 hours of fun.

We must have gone about five miles that way when there came another sound from the back seat. It was the kind of sound that comes with tears.

"I want to go home," she said.

This was all predictable, of course. The only question was how much longer would Dad have to zig-zag back and forth on the busiest stretch of two-lane road in the nation in late July before a decision was made.

I told her we could sure go home, but that I wanted her to think about it for a few more miles because her next decision would be her last.

She thought. She decided. We turned around and headed for home again.

All in all, I was amazed that I remained calm through the whole decision-making process. Maybe it was because I was mellowed by the previous day's camping. Maybe it was because our trip had been so good I didn't want to botch it for both of us by going home angry.

She wiped her tears away. We were going home.

I told her that I felt the same way sometimes, that part of me wanted to be off exploring new places and part of me wanted to be at home with my family.

She thought about that for a minute.

"Yeah," she said. "My legs want to go camping, but my brain wants to go home."

Then she fell into a sleep that lasted all the way to our driveway.

Just a Hint

The night was clear. But more than that, it had a brittle edge to it.

That is why I went for the walk. I pulled on a sweater and descended the back steps into the darkness. I looked at the thermometer on the garage. The face of the thermometer caught just enough light from the kitchen window to be readable.

Fifty-five degrees.

We hadn't seen a 55 in weeks, it seemed. But more than the number made this night different. This 55 had only a trace of accompanying moisture. After a summer full of air thick enough to cut and stack, this was the first night that hinted of Colorado high country or a wood lot in October.

This was air you didn't have to dehumidify before you delivered it to your lungs.

Twice during this early August day I had detected the scent of woodsmoke in the air. In neither case could I find the chimney from which it rose, but it was there, unmistakably. Somebody had fired up the woodstove to chase the morning's chill.

Now the evening was well into dusk. A month ago at this time, the western sky would have been still glowing with remnants of the sunset. But that was a month ago. Things are changing.

My sweater felt good, and I walked with my hands in my pockets. The thin air was intoxicating. As I walked, my mind wandered.

If this first nip in the air affected me this way, I wondered what it meant to the woodcock high in Manitoba. This kind of air, and the shrinking of daylight hours, must have a meaning for woodcock that only woodcock understand. The flight south will be starting soon. And so, a woodcock goes about doing what it needs to get done to be ready.

I wondered the same thing about Canada geese and arctic terns and warblers. Do they welcome the sudden crispness that portends their long journey? Or does the coolness send a shiver of apprehension down their feathered backs? Or do they merely go about their daily business, snatching grass and bugs and mosquitoes, with no hint of what is to come?

I wondered about my friends the dogsledders living on the shores of Great Slave Lake, and about the huskies chained to the posts in their dog yard. Surely a husky cannot ignore that first hint of the coming cold. I could see McLeod or Grayling, waking, stretching, shaking, rattling the chain, yipping and yowling toward the little cabin, yearning to pull again.

And I wondered about my friends' black Labs— Tobie and Moxie and Sally and Kota and Lucky and Rascal. You can't tell me that on their walks on this crisp evening they don't notice the texture of the air. You can't tell me it doesn't quicken their step and touch something deep inside of them that reminds them of rising grouse and running pheasants and cornstalks that clatter in the breeze.

I thought about those things as I watched the crescent moon over garage roofs and baseball diamonds. It was as good-looking a moon as I'd seen in a spell. Thicker than a fingernail moon. Maybe two fingernails. And the color of a pumpkin with a candle inside.

I walked to where I could watch it without garage roofs in the way. It slipped toward a distant ridge of maples. I watched the irregularity of the horizon swallow the glow. Finally, only the tip of the crescent remained. It looked like a porch light half a mile away. When it was gone, I turned to walk home. I was warmed up now. I could take my hands from my pockets.

I am not eager for summer to be passing. But I have tasted the coming fall, and I will be ready.

Like the woodcock and the huskies and the black Labs, I will be ready.

Fall

Spirit of the Hunt

It's coming on. I can feel it.

I am speaking here of the hunt. Not the season itself, you understand. Not merely dates on a calendar. It's the *spirit* of the hunt, the broad canvas waiting to be splashed with the color of our little outings.

That's what's coming on.

I thought maybe I could recapture the feeling or draw some kind of an advance on the season if I went to find it. So, I drove north to what a couple of us refer to as "the old grouse spot." Never mind that it's referred to that way by probably a dozen or two other hunters.

It's our spot.

I was a little startled to see how much logging had taken place there since I'd last walked the old trails in hunting boots. I couldn't find the little trailhead on my first pass. But I spied it the second time, and I went for a little walk.

It didn't feel quite right. The day was warm—even in the shade—and the air felt like a second-grader's breath after a game of tag. The ferns and the grass were still making chlorophyll, and the whole world seemed just a tad too succulent.

But I walked on down the trail hoping I'd flush a grouse or even a woodcock.

I was thinking about the conversations I'd had in the past couple of days. An acquaintance of mine said he was heading north this weekend to build his deer stand. It isn't in prime deer country, and my friend hasn't put a lot of meat in the freezer lately.

"I'm two-for-thirteen," he said, tallying up the years. "But my dad's been hunting there since 1932. Where else are you going to go?"

He wasn't talking so much about shooting deer as he was about fathers and sons and good days in the field—the spirit of the hunt.

Another friend bought himself a county plat book and went exploring new grouse territory this week. He called the other night. He didn't say anything about seeing grouse.

"We put up a six-point buck," he said. "And what are those birds that are all over the road these days? They look like a woodpecker."

He checked his bird book and decided they were common flickers, which they probably were. They're all over the road these days.

A six-point buck. Flickers flushing ahead of the car. That isn't what the grouse hunter had gone to see, but they became part of the fabric of his fall.

Another friend had called me to say he heard that

Browning, the firearms company, was making its Sweet Sixteen 16-gauge shotgun again. Which meant he could order a new barrel for the old Sweet Sixteen he had. Which he did. If you knew the man, you'd know he needs another barrel for a shotgun the way Norman Schwarzkopf needs a new medal.

But the hunt is coming on, and that's part of the way he celebrates the season.

I walked on down the trail, past gone-to-seed fireweed. The ferns brushed my chest, and the grass snagged my shoestrings. When I stopped, blackflies materialized before my eyes.

I wanted the day to be crisp. I wanted a long-sleeved shirt to feel good. I wanted the grasses to smell dry and thin instead of sweet and thick.

It wasn't going to happen. But we're getting there. Any day now, we could wake up to that change of light, that telling breeze, that rustling of leaves. And we'll know.

We'll know the hunt has arrived. For now, though, we'll have to be content just to know it's coming on.

My Stanley

I'm not sure how a grown man can come to be attached to something so heavy and so ugly. But I'll admit it: I love my thermos.

Maybe love is too strong a word. You can't love a thermos bottle in the way you can love a spouse or a hunting dog or a child. But travel with it long enough and you come to appreciate it in a manner reserved for only a few treasured possessions. A good shotgun, or a fly rod, maybe. Or a good pair of boots.

Such a bond is forged with time and use. At the root of the relationship is the simplest of factors: The thing does what it is supposed to do.

My old Stanley thermos does. Mostly I ask it to keep things warm. It does that better than any other thermos

I've ever tossed onto a truck seat or hauled to a duck blind.

Stanleys—now made by the Aladdin company—are the big, gray-green thermoses with the chrome caps and chrome bases. They seem to be made of the same steel that a tank is made from, and they weigh just less than one.

I remember that my grandparents always had a Stanley. I traveled with them as a kid, and though I never drank anything that came out of that thermos, it was always there in the car somewhere.

I should have known to get a Stanley when I grew up; my grandparents always owned things that worked.

But in what turned out to be short-sighted efforts to save money or weight, I bought several thermoses before the Stanley. I can still remember the shattering of the fragile liners when one of the pre-Stanley bottles would roll out of the car door. The moment of destruction always sounded like a light bulb exploding on the pavement.

Finally, in a pre-duck-hunting frenzy one year, I decided it was time to get a good thermos. I was leaving the next morning for five days in South Dakota.

I headed for the neighborhood drugstore, knowing I would likely have to pay top dollar. I cruised the aisles until I found the thermoses. There it was. The quart-size Stanley, big and heavy and—on sale. Normally $32. Now $22. It was meant to be.

That was five or six years ago, and since then I've hauled that thermos all over the place. I strapped a plastic handle on it to control the roll factor, and I've since wrapped camouflage tape around the chrome portions of the bottle in the hope of spooking fewer mallards. The smooth green sides of the bottle are now flecked and flaked from encounters with dogsleds and truck floors and canoe bottoms.

But it still works.

Once I left it in the truck nearly full of tea while I went duck hunting in the canoe country for two days and one night. When I came back to the truck, the tea was still warm. Not hot, but warm. Not bad.

I have come to appreciate the old thermos as it lies on the seat beside me, while I head north somewhere in the car. We've seen a lot of North Shore sunrises together. I've poured a lot of cups of tea by the dome light of the truck in the black of an October morning while I've headed for a duck blind.

But I never appreciate the thermos more than when I'm out there—in the blind or on the trail or at the tailgate. That's when you need what's inside the thermos—when the rain is boot-sole deep on the canoe floor, when you've come 15 miles from your last camp on some frozen lake or when your fingers are so cold you can barely make them pull another shotgun shell from your vest pocket.

That's when I reach for the old thermos. I unscrew that little green plug. And I pour myself something that warms my body from the inside out.

Deer Camp

The hunters had come back.

Their boots squished in the wet leaves on the forest floor as they approached the clearing. It was like finding an old friend. Nothing had changed since last year.

The rusted frame of the logging-camp bed was still twisted beneath the hazel trees. The trail that led south to the swamp was still discernible. The blackened coals of last year's last campfire lay cold and wet under the balsams.

It was a modest place. But it was deer camp.

These hunters could have been any of hundreds on this October weekend. This camp could have been any of thousands that dot Minnesota's North Woods.

This is the time of year when deer hunters retreat to

their hunting grounds. Not to hunt, not yet, but to see what another year has brought.

These are the deer hunters nobody sees, for they don't wear the blaze orange of November. The pickup they leave at the edge of the road might be that of just another grouse hunter for all the passers-by know. The smoke from the shack could just as well be that of a summer cabin owner, warding off the chill during one last week-end before closing the place up.

The deer hunters who go to camp in October relish this anonymity. They need not be part of a greater experience now. They will get enough of that later on.

This is a weekend of quiet reflection, a time to rekindle memories of camps past. It is best done over simple tasks like repairing a door latch or lashing up the deer pole or splitting some wood.

A hunter's mind wanders at times like this. He thinks about when he first started coming up to camp. How he'd dreamed of coming for years before his dad finally let him. How quickly the years had gone by since then. And how it had been so tough coming back the year his dad didn't.

Now his own son and daughter are begging to come along. It sounds funny hearing himself say the same words to them his father had said to him all those years ago. He'll know when the time is right, he tells himself. And he knows how special it will be for them the first time.

In the afternoon, the hunters will take a walk. They'll take their shotguns along in case they put up a grouse. But they won't care if they see one or not.

They'll be looking for deer sign. Deep, almond-shaped points in the rain-softened soil. Nipped stems of red osier dogwood. Droppings under the sapling dogwood and aspen.

Perhaps, if the bucks have begun to think about mating, the hunters will see the shredded bark where antlers have been rubbed against the trees. Nearby, the forest duff might be bared where a buck has pawed his defiance at those who would come behind him.

The hunters will note all of this, maybe even log the information on a tattered topographic map with a stubby pencil back at the shack. They will fire up the stove, heat up a simple meal and talk about possible November strategies based on their October afternoon's walk.

Sometime late the next day, they'll load up and leave the deer camp. They'll take a good feeling with them.

It's always that way when you've revisited an old friend.

A Touch of Wildness

He has been through this a thousand times.

Why he hunts.

Why, in a time and place when it is far from essential to go out and get wild meat to feed his family, and in spite of something within himself that has asked him if this activity is really so important, he keeps doing it.

It isn't that he hasn't tried other diversions. Sport seems to be the closest to meeting his needs. Marathon cross-country skiing. Long-distance running. They provide much of what he seeks. Training. Testing physical limits. Finding emotional release. Reaching physical accomplishment beyond what he had thought might be possible.

But he has left most of the endurance sports behind, at least for now. And still he hunts.

He will hunt again this fall, he knows. As surely as the sun begins to kiss the popples at an angle that signals September, as surely as the nights edge toward crispness, he will go again.

All of the sounds and scents and scenes come flickering through his mind. The clicking of a Labrador's toenails landing lightly on a pickup tailgate. A wet canoe, a thermos of hot chocolate, a sky segmented by cattail fronds. A leaf-strewn path defined by ranks of naked aspen.

Those are the tangibles. He can explain those.

What he cannot get at so easily is the wildness the hunt gives him. The part beyond the pickups and the coats and the duck calls is why he keeps hunting.

As managed as today's hunts are, as regimented as they can be by deadlines and schedules and regulations, as comfortable as they can be made by synthetic fabrics and mostly dry boots, a wildness still emerges from the hunt that he finds nowhere else.

He doesn't always rediscover it the first day out. Or even the second. He has to wear away the sense of tidiness and order he brought with him from the city. He has to get dirty and not care about it. He has to ache and have the ache go away and then go hunt again.

But that is only part of where the wildness comes from. The rest of it comes from the critters and the country.

He feels it most keenly when a rooster pheasant leads him, behind the dog, through the cattails and into the weed cover and along the slough until finally it is up, pulsating on the rise, tailfeathers quivering, the big bird a slash of color against the prairie sky.

He wants to bring the rooster down, but he might or might not. He gets some. He misses some. What is important is that he has lived with that bird for the past 10 minutes, run its runways, read its mind, wondered at its sheer unpredictability and its knack for staying alive.

Sometimes he and the dog will run like that for a quarter mile or more, hot on scent, and no bird will materialize. It is long gone. He and the dog stand there, panting, knowing they have been foxed. Again.

He accepts that. It is part of the wildness.

The deer hunter knows the wildness, too, but it's a quiet kind of wild. The kind that comes with sitting in the rain or the sleet or the parka-stabbing cold, listening to the flutter of chickadee wings, watching a woolen sky and sniffing great forestfuls of rotting aspen leaves.

And wondering. Wondering about the wind and the mating habits of whitetails and the power of his—the hunter's—own body scent and what blaze orange camouflage looks like through a buck's eyes. Wondering if today is the day or if it is merely another in the dues-paying process. Wondering at the tenacity with which a whitetail clings to life against the odds of cold and snow and wind and timber wolves—and, yes, 16 days in November.

He knows, the hunter does, that all of this is recreational, that modern hunting is a privilege and an exercise. Rooster pheasants or not, whitetail buck or not, the house or the cabin or the truck will be waiting. This is not the Eskimo and the polar bear and survival. This is not the Pilgrims and the first Thanksgiving.

But it seems important, at least to this hunter, to remember that the hunt wasn't always recreational. Football was always football. A game. Baseball was always baseball. A pastime. But hunting, even today, is linked to a time when it mattered if you knew the country, if you could get by on the land, if you could shoot straight and take care of your game.

We haven't spent enough years on concrete and asphalt to have that bred out of us, he guesses. And so, on some level, it still matters to him that he does it right. That he can move quietly in the forest. That he can look at a piece of country and say, yes, there are likely some birds there. That he can walk all day if he must.

When the hunt is over, that knowledge is what he takes with him. He takes it back to a world in which something like making money, which shouldn't matter, does matter.

He'll punch in. He'll play his role in the civilized world.

And know that inside of him—the hunter—is a touch of wildness he won't let die.

Duck Camp

Birch leaves drifted to the ground on a northwest wind. Frost etched sumac leaves in the woods. Two black Labradors tussled in the grass.

Tom Bell stood in the morning quiet, listening to the leaves rattle on this opening day of duck season.

"Isn't this the way it's supposed to be?" he asked.

It was shortly after 9:00 A.M. It was Saturday. Bell was standing next to a two-story frame home on the shores of a pothole pond not far from Squaw Lake northwest of Grand Rapids. You would call the place a home. Bell said a dozen or more other duck hunters call it simply "duck camp."

In a few hours, our party would shove off in camouflaged boats and scoot across the 10-acre puddle. We'd hunker in the sumacs and hope to shoot ducks.

That is what Duluth hunters have been doing at this camp for six decades, as near as anyone can figure.

Because duck season doesn't open until noon on opening day, there was plenty of time to get ready on Saturday morning. Time to go flush some grouse. Time to shovel sandy soil on the new water line to the house. Time for one Lab, Briar, to get reacquainted with another Lab, Kenna. Time to string new anchor line on some bluebill decoys.

Tantalizing aromas were wafting from the kitchen, where Meg Goelzer, the camp cook and caretaker, was doing something memorable with bacon and eggs. There would be the traditional camp breakfast before anyone left to hunt ducks.

Bell had it figured right. This was the way it was supposed to be.

We acknowledged our concerns about the continental flight of ducks being near an all-time low. Those concerns would compel some of us to sit out future hunts. Even for this hunt we agreed that hen mallards were off-limits.

But this still was duck season. It looked like duck season. It felt like duck season. And the northwest wind that had been blowing for two days was said to have brought a lot of ring-necked ducks into Northern Minnesota.

The prospects of seeing some of those ducks from noon to the 4:00 P.M. close of shooting hours had spread an air of optimism through this camp.

At 11:00 A.M., hip boots, camouflage jackets and shell bags were gathered, and we moved to the lake. Most of us would string out along The Pass, a low spit of land between the pothole and a larger lake to the north.

Ducks almost always used The Pass when leaving the little lake.

Dozens of decoys were set out as hunters reached their blinds. It was beginning to look a lot more like duck season.

Minnesota duck seasons begin at noon mostly to conserve ducks, the thought being that a sunrise shoot on opening morning would put a lot more ducks in the bag and drive a lot more ducks out of the state. A noon opener, being better for the ducks, is often not so good for those who hunt them.

But this day had promise. A few lesser scaup—blue-bills—whistled past shortly before noon, and two mallards swung low over a weedy beach on the adjoining lake.

At noon, the hunkering started. From the distance came the sound of gunshots, like firecrackers set off inside 55-gallon drums.

Over the course of the next four hours, ducks were moving nearly all the time. Some high. Some low. Some low but wide.

"Mark!" the cry would come.

And a pair of goldeneyes or a single bluebill or a single ring-necked duck would come too close on his decoy inspection.

By all counts, it was an opener worth waiting for. The shooting was good. The retrieving was good. Even the missing was good. When plenty of ducks are flying, the missing never hurts as much.

As good as the shooting was, Tom Bell knew the best part of the day was yet to come. It had come on many other days, whether the shooting was good or poor or somewhere in between.

It always came late in the afternoon, when it was time

to load up wet dogs and old shotguns and head for camp. That, more than the ducks, is what keeps Bell coming back here.

"It's the smoke coming out of the stone chimney," he said. "It's the light coming out of the windows. It's the flicker of the fireplace fire reflecting in the main room. It's the pine trees you see going way over the cabin, and the geese you see flying over when you're coming in at night. It's the hum of the people around there.

"It's a warmth that warms you right straight through."

Ask any duck hunter. Isn't that the way it's supposed to be?

Winter

Arctic Wolves
Sticky Business
Jackpine Bob
Northern Passages

Arctic Wolves

I looked out the window of the Twin Otter and gazed past the wing onto a berg of ice bathed in the glow of the midnight sun.

I had been following our progress on a map as best I could. I figured we were just off Axel Heiberg Island in the High Arctic. The Otter was headed north. To the top of the world—the North Pole.

We were approaching Eureka, an outpost and weather station on Ellesmere Island. We would refuel there—one of two refueling stops we would have to make on the way to the pole from Resolute Bay, Northwest Territories.

Since early March at this latitude—82 degrees north—the sun had not set. It circled the top of the world each day, tracing a halo around the arctic. At about midnight each day, it would dip slightly toward the northern horizon. But it would do no more than a touch-and-go landing, rise again and begin another low-level circuit.

From our plane, at 10,000 feet, even the arctic looked warm and soft in that diagonal light. Outside, the temperature was somewhere between 10 below and zero, but the light was all peach and salmon and pink. Only long blue shadows of the rugged cliffs and inland peaks looked the color of cold.

When we landed at Eureka, the pilot shut down only one of the plane's two engines. Bush pilots don't like to put themselves in a position where they might need a jump start.

We were no sooner on the ground than Jim Brandenburg, a National Geographic photographer who also was on the flight, motioned me his way.

"Want to go see some wolves?" he asked.

We would be at Eureka for about half an hour. I didn't hesitate.

"Follow me," Brandenburg said.

Brandenburg, a fellow-Minnesotan who had been on Ellesmere before, had photographed everything from the island's snowshoe hares to its muskoxen.

Lugging a camera bag full of Nikons and lenses, Brandenburg took off down the gravel runway at a trot. We were both dressed for the cold, in parkas, wind pants and pile caps.

Soon Brandenburg veered from the runway and dropped onto the raw tundra. There was little snow, and what there was had been tortured by the arctic winds. It was crusted, sculpted and fluted into sharp-edged designs. In many places, the ground had been blown bare, and leathery stems of tundra grasses poked toward the sky.

Everywhere, it seemed, small dark ovals dotted the snow. I bent for a closer look. I could only assume they were muskoxen droppings. So scoured was the landscape that mini-drifts would form downwind of single droppings. The drifts were as hard and crusty as day-old toast.

Suddenly, Brandenburg stopped. He pointed at something large and dark in front of us. He said nothing.

The object was a muskox skull, horns still intact. There were no signs of the rest of the animal except for a rib cage, picked clean. Wolves had dined here. And foxes. And perhaps ravens.

Brandenburg began trotting again, down a long slope. The country was treeless, of course, and seemed to roll on forever. We were on the edge of a broad valley. Below us lay an expanse of white—a frozen inlet from the ocean or possibly a lake.

I was looking out across the valley, running alongside Brandenburg. The landing strip was far above us now, and the weather station and refueling depot were out of sight.

Then, from below us, it appeared. A wolf. Rangy and yellow-white, it rose into our view from behind a ridge that was below us. It was trotting, and it kept trotting after it saw us.

It was not the kind of wolf one is accustomed to seeing in the North Woods of Minnesota. Minnesota's wolves are usually buff to gray to charcoal. They are always larger than you expect them to be. This wolf was something entirely different.

If not a wolf it might have been a thoroughbred colt.

It seemed to be all legs. It covered ground effortlessly, flicking its legs at the ankles, eating up tundra in an easy trot.

The wolf's fur was long and shaggy. The wolf would be shedding its winter coat soon. Though heavily furred, the animal looked lean and sinewy, fit to cover the tundra for 20 or 30 miles a day.

The wolf stared at us as it moved, first laterally and then in a wide arc behind us. It was perhaps a hundred yards away.

Brandenburg stopped as soon as the wolf appeared. He looked directly at the animal, and turned as it began to circle behind us. He rocked his head back and began to howl.

Then the others appeared, one at a time, over the same ridge where the first had materialized. Two, three, four of them. Then another, and another. They followed the first in single file, each a comfortable distance from those ahead and behind it.

It was sometime after two in the morning in the High Arctic, and a pack of wolves was circling us and Brandenburg was howling.

Why not? I leaned back and cut loose with my best howl.

I thought we sounded good, Brandenburg and I, but the wolves never answered to offer an objective comparison.

They circled us once, every head turned our way. It was a large circle, and I have no idea how long we stood there, turning slowly at its hub, watching the wolves. I felt no fear, probably because I figured my partner knew these animals, and maybe they knew him.

I know only that for those few minutes, I was transported to another level of appreciation for the universe we call home. The country was immense, and it might have been miles between us and the next wild, living things. And just beyond our reach were the wolves, moving, watching, at home in this unforgiving country, getting by, surviving, with apparent ease.

I never felt a sense of hunter-and-hunted during the encounter. I didn't feel at any time that the wolves considered Brandenburg and me their next meal. Nor did I wish I had a gun.

I felt an unfamiliar peace in letting the whole scene unfold, in letting happen whatever would happen.

The lead wolf had made nearly a complete circle around us when, with no wasted motion, he simply crested a small ridge and dropped out of sight. One by one, the other wolves followed, until Brandenburg and I were left alone on the tundra.

We stopped howling. Brandenburg looked at me and smiled.

We hustled back to catch a plane for the North Pole.

Sticky Business

It seemed like your basic Thanksgiving dinner. I'm not sure how we got to talking about people's tongues getting stuck to cold metal.

Eight or 10 of us were gathered around the table. Even before everyone else had told a tongue-stuck-to-metal story, I realized I was a minority of one.

I couldn't believe it: I was the only one who had never succumbed to the temptation to lick a sub-freezing chunk of steel.

I started asking around. In the office. At a couple of parties. On the street. It seems that almost every kid who grew up north of the Iowa line has, at one time or another, licked a piece of metal in January.

Oh, these people had heard the horror stories before

they tried it. They'd heard about bloodied tongues and pieces of lips left on downspouts until the spring thaw.

But they went ahead and did it anyway. It seems like getting fused to a cold piece of pipe is a mandatory ritual in the North Country. Sort of like your first pair of Sorels.

What people have become stuck to is limited only by the imagination—and territorial boundaries—of a seven-year-old. I talked to people who had latched onto tether-ball poles, street sign posts, stop signs, hand railings, chain link fences, basketball goal standards, swing sets and door knobs. Oh, and a dog kennel.

My favorite story was Ken's.

He was standing next to a street sign with a buddy, waiting for a school bus. For some reason known only to grade-schoolers, Ken decided to see if his tongue would stick to the sign post, and—wouldn't you know it—it did. He was still attached when the bus rolled up.

Ken's buddy, seeing no other options, simply reached out and karate chopped Ken's tongue off the post. Part of the tongue stayed on the post, but Ken got to school on time.

After researching this subject I began to feel as if I weren't a complete person, having never been stuck to anything cold.

Well, I was at a gathering of friends the other night, and the time seemed right. My friend Ken was there. He could see the desire in my eyes. He knew I was ready for this passage into Minnesotanhood.

"We could go outside right now," he said.

I deliberated only a second. I was ready. But I'm not dumb. I filled a coffee cup with warm water so Ken could liberate me without karate once I had engaged the metal.

It was a nice December night. Nine degrees. Lots of stars. We left the chatter of the party behind us and walked out to a galvanized steel clothesline pole.

Ken was chuckling.

I licked two fingers and touched them to the pole, sort of like putting your toes in the lake to test the water. My fingers stuck reasonably well. I figured a tongue, being wetter and warmer, would work better.

I leaned over and licked.

It was a magnetic sensation, so quickly did my tongue adhere to the metal. Ken liked this a lot. I remained in link-up with the clothesline pole for a few seconds. Then the heat of my tongue warmed the metal, and I was able to pull free.

Too easy.

I wasn't going to settle for a token effort at tongue-sticking. If I was going to become a Minnesotan, I was going to do it right.

We moved to a steel step railing for another attempt. I walked up to the railing. It was wide and flat. It looked cold.

"You gotta get a lot of your tongue on it," Ken said.

It's wonderful to have supportive friends at these critical times in one's life.

I slathered up a juicy tongueful of saliva and slapped my tongue on the railing. We had contact. We had a hook-up. This was the real thing.

You know it's the real thing when you hear yourself saying, "Aaaauuuuuhhhhhh."

Which meant, "Hit me with the water, Ken."

Ken, of course, was convulsed with laughter. He hadn't begun to think about freeing me. He was having too much fun. He was also, he confessed later, thinking about going inside to call more spectators out.

When I said "Aaaauuuuuhhhhhh" again and started pointing at my tongue, he only laughed harder. I could see I was on my own.

It's hard to say how long I was fast to that railing. Thirty seconds? A minute?

I tried to lean back, but all I could feel was my tongue being pulled out of my mouth. Finally, I leaned closer to the railing and did some heavy breathing. I warmed the metal enough that I could peel my tongue away, one taste bud at a time.

Finally, the last tender piece of tongue popped free.

I stood back, relieved. I moved my tongue around inside my mouth. It felt the way it feels the day after you've taken a big bite of a pizza that was too hot to eat. Sort of raw and desensitized.

But I felt great. I felt proud. I had done it. I had licked cold steel.

Ken was almost through laughing. He reached out his big paw to me and shook my hand.

"Congratulations," he said.

"Thanks," I said. "I feel like I'm a real Minnesotan now."

He just smiled.

"Have you ever had lutefisk?" he asked.

Jackpine Bob

He came skidding around the corner on his cross-country skis and coasted to a halt where the driveway met the sidewalk.

His face was flushed. His limbs were loose. His eyes were bright and clear.

The temperature was 20 below zero.

No matter, Bob Cary had needed a ski workout. He had zipped over to Jasper Lake, not far from his home in the woods near Ely. He had skate-skied a quick five-mile loop. Now back home, he flipped his ski bindings open and stepped out of them.

"One thing about this weather," he said. "Keeps the mosquitoes down."

He picked up his skis and hustled to the house.

At 68, "Jackpine Bob" Cary has shown no signs of gearing down.

He has eight cross-country ski races on his schedule. He also will put in his two days a week as editor of the *Ely Echo*, do some free-lance outdoors writing, try to get his third book sold to a publisher, crank out illustrations for books and magazines and make his annual canoe trip to Quetico Provincial Park with Lil, his wife of more than 40 years.

None of that, of course, will be permitted to interfere with his fishing.

It was the fishing that drew Bob and Lil to the North when Bob was outdoors editor for the *Chicago Daily News* in the '50s and '60s. The prospect of being closer to good fishing was the catalyst for their move from Illinois to Ely in 1966.

"I'd have gotten here quicker if I knew it was here," Cary says. "I grew up with corn and soybeans."

After operating a canoe outfitting business on Moose Lake near Ely for eight years, the Carys sold the business. Bob hooked up with the fledgling *Echo* in 1974 and has been there two days a week since. He writes his weekly quip, "View from the North Country" by Jackpine Bob, plus a column, news stories and editorials.

"To most people, Bob Cary is the *Echo*," says owner and publisher Anne Wognum.

Through Cary's visibility at the *Echo* he has emerged as something of a North Woods character. To the public, he is "Jackpine Bob"—part columnist, part standup comic, part woodsman.

But to those who know him, he is more than that.

"People think of him as a comedian, and he is. He

entertains us," says his friend, Patti Steger of Ely. "But there's a depth to him."

"I think of him as a very genuine person," says Hank Goodsky, a Chippewa Indian who taught Cary the Ojibwe language.

Behind Cary the storyteller and Cary the witty columnist is another man—a humbled combat veteran, self-taught naturalist, a student of Chippewa culture and a homespun philosopher who holds a holistic view of the planet.

Cary grew up during the Depression in rural Joliet, Illinois. His dad taught him to fish, and a neighbor boy taught him to hunt and trap. That and a few summers at his Aunt Nellie's cottage, where he discovered an 18-foot Old Town canoe, were all it took to hook him on the outdoors.

After high school, Cary studied journalism for two years at a community college. Then World War II broke out, and he enlisted in the Marines.

"That was one of the more radical aberrations of my life," he says.

He saw more action than he wanted to in the South Pacific. Thousands of American soldiers died around him in heavy fighting on the islands of Guadalcanal, Tarawa, Saipan and Tianan. He was terrified most of the time, and the senselessness of war stunned him.

"It's the most complete insanity the human mind ever dreamed up."

He bounced from island to island and found himself back in the States—alive—in 1945.

"I was very lucky to get out of that thing. It was like being in a rapids you shouldn't have been in and making it through. I thought, 'From now on, ain't nothin' gonna bother this cat. This is all overtime.'

"What's really important is that you're here. You only make this trip once."

That is the spirit that has guided Cary through the rest of his life. He'll take a stand. He'll fight for what he believes. But he won't allow himself to become bitter. At some point in any battle, he'll step back, smile and come at it with a fresh perspective.

"He's so progressive, so forward-thinking," says his friend Steger. "He has such a big picture in his head. You don't find that in many people. He has all the history and humanity rolled into it."

It seems Cary sorted out early the important things in life. He never has made a lot of money, but he always has made the most of life. He made only four thousand dollars a year at the *Chicago Daily News*, and had to moonlight as editor of a weekly paper in Joliet. But he traveled all over North America fishing and hunting.

He had married Lil Kluge, a professional musician who played bass fiddle in a dance combo, in 1948.

In the late 1940s and early '50s, Cary did freelance wildlife illustrations, worked in wildlife research, painted houses, produced an outdoors radio show— "anything to make a buck."

While he was moonlighting for the Joliet weekly paper, Cary stumbled onto a news story involving the Mafia. He received a death threat and began carrying a handgun to work. Once the dailies picked up the story, the heat was off, but the incident got him to thinking about how he wanted to live life.

"That helped get me up here," he said. "I got a little tired of playing footsie with those people."

When Ely's Emery Bulinski offered him a proposition to start an outfitting business, Bob and Lil loaded the

U-Haul and drove north. With Bulinski's financial backing and a piece of property on Moose Lake, the Carys built Canadian Border Outfitters from scratch.

They were in paradise.

"We came up here because it was still wild and natural, even though it had been logged over and burned a few times," Cary said. "There were a lot of lakes with a lot of fish."

Bob and Lil built a successful business with Bulinski's backing. After eight years, they sold their half-interest back to Bulinski. It was 1974. Bob and Lil wanted to slow down and simplify their lives—and go fishing.

Which, more or less, is what they've done since.

Five days a week, depending on the season, Cary fishes, skis, hunts, puts up firewood and does writing and illustrating.

Carl Raglin has been camping and fishing with Cary for 15 years. "I've never seen a guy catch fish like Bob Cary," Raglin says. "I almost believe he could get fish out of a bathtub."

The other two days of the week—every Thursday and Friday—Cary is at the *Ely Echo*. It isn't for the money. He makes a hundred dollars a week there. He receives no benefits except use of the phone—something the Carys do without at home.

He writes his *Birdshot and Backlashes*, hunting and fishing column. He also turns out his *View from the North Country* for the paper's front page. He writes news stories and editorials.

His news stories are solid but not award-winners. His humor occasionally is perceived as chauvinistic. On the whole, however, his wit is the product of a nimble mind that often brings together diverse elements with poignant effect.

He makes his readers think. And smile.

In the past dozen years, Cary has written two books, *The Big Wilderness Canoe Manual* and *Winter Camping.* He also has done illustrations for five other hardcover books. He has written free-lance stories and done free-lance illustrations for many magazines.

He and Lil share a simple one-bedroom home in the woods east of Ely. Lil designed the home, and they built it together with help from friends. They live frugally, getting by comfortably on Social Security income, interest from savings plans and Bob's salary at the newspaper. Most of their meat comes from the woods.

Bob balances time in his studio with his pursuit of fitness. At 6-foot-1 and 170 pounds, he is whippet-lean and healthy.

"As far as I know, I'm fine. But you run into these things all the time in the obituaries: 'He was fine until yesterday.' "

Lil was diagnosed with ovarian cancer in 1987 and fought through two operations and 10 months of chemotherapy before receiving a clean bill of health. Some say it was the only time they have seen Bob shaken.

"You realize that forever ain't forever," he says.

He and Lil enjoy a close relationship. Clearly, they are each other's best friends. They enjoy each other's company in a canoe, on the dance floor or simply at the dinner table while sharing a venison supper.

"They have such a unique and special relationship, full of care and concern and good humor," said *Echo* publisher Wognum. "It's impossible to think about Bob without thinking about Lilly."

There is a gentleness and peace to Cary that isn't always apparent to his readers or those who find themselves an audience for his storytelling jags. His recent study of the Chippewa culture, and perhaps simply his growing older, have refined his philosophy. He seems more willing, at least in small groups, to discuss those kinds of thoughts than he did even a few years ago.

He studied Ojibwe under Hank Goodsky, a Chippewa Indian and an Ojibwe instructor at the University of Minnesota-Duluth.

"I see Bob as a person who understands, who is really appreciative of the language," Goodsky said. "I see him as one of my best students. My mother, who passed away three months ago, she thought highly of him. She called him *akwenzii*. It means, in a good way, old man. A man of high esteem."

Cary's appreciation of Indian ways has blended well with his own philosophy.

"An Indian told me once, 'One of the differences between us and you is that the white man says, "This land belongs to me." The Indian says, "I belong to the land." ' That spells it all out.

"You see, we're a part of the land, and the worst we can do as a people is to get too far from the land.

"As you get older, you realize you have a responsibility to this old mudball we live on. It's not enough to make a living. You have a responsibility to leave it better for the next generation. It's like tidying up the campsite when you leave."

But don't try to talk to Cary about leaving the campsite yet.

"The first thing is, I ain't goin'."

Then he relents—momentarily.

"But if I *was* gonna go, they could throw my ashes in the woods. Cook me up and throw me in the woods. Not in the lake—I been fightin' pollution all my life. Put me in the woods, where it'll do some good. Maybe help something grow."

To help out in the unlikely event he would go, Cary has written his epitaph already. He says it should read:

> *I could have been eminently famous in a number of different fields, but every time I was about to do something great, I went fishing.*

He smiles.
"I never regretted the fishing," he says.
Jackpine Bob.
Akwenzii.

Northern Passages

My early northern passages were made with paddle and packsack, or on the runners of a dogsled or a pair of cross-country skis.

I was new in this country—the North Woods—and I couldn't get enough of it. I wanted to fill in the blank spots on my maps, make the portages I had heard about, follow rivers to Hudson Bay, know how it felt to sleep under the shimmer of northern lights.

My partners and I were drawn sometimes by the promise of walleyes or lake trout, but just as often by the sheer adventure of seeing what was around the next bend.

We did find some walleyes and lake trout. We made camps where the spirit of the voyageurs danced in our fires. We came to know mosquitoes and blackflies, good sled dogs and cold nights, wild rivers and big lakes.

The passages weren't always easy. At times we found ourselves thigh-deep in bogs, or desperate for the lee of the next island on a windswept lake or pushing after dark behind a team of dogs. But it didn't matter. We were young people in new country, and we weren't pushing ourselves so much as we were being pulled along by the country itself.

Now, though, some of that has changed. Our passages aren't always those of the paddle and path; instead they're the passages of life—having children, waking up and finding ourselves in the middle of life, watching friendships mature, wondering what the years ahead hold for us.

When we had our first child a few years ago, I remember telling friends that, no, our lives haven't changed. We still camp. We still fish. We still paddle and portage.

That much was true. We do many of the things we once did, but we do them for different reasons. At a different pace. With new rewards.

One thing hasn't changed. We're still experiencing these new passages in our lives against the backdrop of the North. It means something to me that our six-year-old knows the call of the barred owl, that she reports with excitement each April that the peepers are peeping again, that she can fall asleep as easily in a canoe as in her own bed.

I find, these days, all of that matters more than whether I have caught walleyes.

I never thought it would be this way. I never thought I'd find myself four days into a week-long trip and fighting an intense desire to be at home, rocking a one-year-old to bed.

It never occurred to me that going back to a familiar camp on a familiar lake with a good friend would mean as much to me as coming to know a new piece of the map. But it does.

Passages. They slip up on you like a morning fog on a canoe-country lake in September. Like a full moon, there, before you know it, over Lake Superior. Like the smell of woodsmoke, drifting down the lake from your camp when you're paddling back at dusk.

I'm not sure what new discoveries are ahead of me. I'm not sure I'll be ready for them, or that I'll even recognize them as they unfold.

But I think I know how I'll find them. I'll be shuffling along some portage trail, trying to appreciate a patch of bunchberries while the yoke of the canoe bites into my shoulders. I'll be sliding into a cold sleeping bag on a February night, listening to sled dogs jangling the stake-out chain outside the tent. I'll be gazing up from the water at a cluster of Indian rock paintings, marveling at this country that has changed so little in so many centuries.

That's where I'll be. Finding new passages. Here in the North.

Sam Cook has been the outdoors writer for the *Duluth News-Tribune* since 1980. His travels have taken him canoeing to Hudson Bay, dogsledding in the Northwest Territories, and paddling the Quetico–Superior wilderness. He is author of the books *Quiet Magic, Friendship Fires,* and *Up North,* all available from the University of Minnesota Press. He lives with his family in Duluth, Minnesota.